Behind the Door of Deceit

Understanding the Biggest Liars in
Our Lives

Bella DePaulo, Ph.D.

2009

2

CONTENTS

Introduction

PART 1: Stories from the Dupes

1. *Lies about love and sex*................................**11**
2. *Deadly lies*...**25**
3. *Lies that are a matter of honor*.......................**33**
4. *Whose flesh and blood? Lies about kinship*...........**37**
5. *Lies about fortune and livelihood*....................**39**

PART 2: Deeper into Deceit

6. *The why and how of serious lies, and what happens
   afterwards*..**43**

PART 3: Stories from the Liars

7. *The most primitive lie: Avoiding punishment and
   blame*...**65**
8. *Entitlement lies: Lying for what you think you deserve*...**74**
9. *Instrumental lies*....................................**78**
10. *Lies about passions*..................................**81**
11. *Identity lies: Becoming a different person*...........**86**
12. *Taking a fall: Lies told to cover for someone else*......**96**
13. *Living a lie*...**101**

PART 4: Lessons for Liars and Dupes

14. *Tips for turning down the heat on deceit*............**104**

About the Author....................................**134**

3

Introduction

When my colleagues and I first came up with the bright idea of asking dozens of perfect strangers to tell a team of psychologists all about their most profound lies, we weren't at all sure that we wouldn't get laughed off the planet. But tell us they did. Men and women, Black and White, gay and straight, students and senior citizens, and just about everyone else in between and beyond those categories – all of those Americans talked. All together, we gathered more than 200 stories of the most serious lies ever told to our participants, and the most serious lies ever told to them. We started by recruiting more than 60 college students; they are rather accustomed to strange requests. When they didn't flinch, then we headed beyond the gates of academia to the community to talk to a more diverse sampling of liars and dupes.

When we began this research, we thought that the kinds of lies people would describe in response to the two questions – the worst lie they ever told, and the worst lie anyone ever told to them – would be about the same. They were not. When people related their experiences as dupes--that is, when they described the lies that were told *to* them by someone else, they told tales of big, important, emotionally-charged life issues. Their stories were about love and sex; death, illness, and violence; honor and kinship; fortune and livelihood. When instead they described their experiences as liars--that is, when they described the lies that they had told to others, they more often told us about smashing the car, running errands on company time, and telling mom about their quiet evening with their friends instead of their passionate adventures in the back of a car on an old country road.

The people who shared their experiences with big-time deceit first simply told us their stories in their own words. Then we asked them more and more questions. For example: Why lie? How did it feel? How did the deceit come undone (if it ever did)? Now what?

I'll start with the stories from the dupes – the people who talked about getting deceived in a big way. Then the lie-tellers will get my attention. At the end, I will offer a psychological guide to those who would like to be lied to less often, or who want to learn how to refrain from telling serious lies themselves, or who are looking for suggestions as to how to "come clean" about a lie they have already told.

In these pages, I will refer often to my collaborators. They are Matthew Ansfield, Susan Kirkendol, and Joe Boden. Many thanks to them. We published an academic report of our research on serious lies in the journal *Basic and Applied Social Psychology* in 2004. Professional journals put a premium on brevity, and so our report only included the most basic descriptions of the lies, with no extensive quotes. In this book, I restore the voices to the many people who so graciously shared their stories of the most serious lies in their lives. I've changed their names and some of the other details of their stories. Otherwise, though, the quotes highlighted in the boxes and in the text are their own words. I am tremendously grateful to all of these people. They have taught me a lot, and now I hope you will feel enlightened by them as well.

PART 1

Stories from the Dupes

1. Lies about love and sex

2. Deadly lies

3. Lies that are a matter of honor

4. Whose flesh and blood? Lies about kinship

5. Lies about fortune and livelihood

Chapter 1

Lies About Love and Sex

In 1970 my former husband, who was the Dean of a college, became involved with a secretary in the Provost's office. My former husband is an ordained minister and before becoming a college dean, he had been a professor in the Religion Department of a different university. We had been married nearly 20 years at the time, had four terrific children, and I thought our marriage was basically happy. This affair was the last thing I would have expected of him.

The lie was actually a whole series of lies and evasions. The one that I remember most clearly is that he told me that the demands of his new job required him to go back to his office after dinner nearly every night. Often he would not come home until 1 or 2 in the morning. Since working hours like this was typical of him (he has always been a night person), I was not suspicious. I didn't like being alone every night, but I never suspected

11

that another woman, and not the office, was his destination. His manner toward me during that period was not noticeably different. He is not a warm, outgoing person, and had often gone for days without saying very much. I knew he was worried about his work, especially his relationship with the Provost. The whole thing blew up when he returned from a business trip. I was collecting his dirty clothes for the laundry, when I noticed a small jewelry box in his briefcase. I was curious and opened it, and it contained a lovely pendant on a chain. When he traveled, he typically brought back gifts for me and the children, and I thought he had bought it for me. I returned it to its box. The next night we attended a play at the college. During intermission we met the secretary in the theater lobby, and around her neck was the pendant. I'm not the type to make a public scene, but I quietly demanded that we leave, and once outside, confronted him with it.

Suddenly, I was hearing that he had been unhappy for years and was thinking of leaving me. At the time I was a very different person than I am now, and I felt as if my whole world had fallen away beneath me.

Six years later I sued for divorce. The lie (and the affair, long since over) were not the cause of it, but they were the spur that caused me to look at my marriage in a way I never had, up to   that point. The next few years were very painful ones, but I gradually, with the help of some very fine counselors, took control of my life. Today I'm a very happy lady, married for three years to a wonderful guy who is my closest friend as well as husband. He is direct and outspoken and I know that if I do something that displeases him, I'll hear about it now, not in 15 years!"

—Rita

Even though lying is bad, it's worse toward the people you love.

Before my colleagues and I started studying serious lies, we were trying to understand the little lies that people tell in their everyday lives. We asked people in those previous studies to keep a diary, every day for a week, of all of their social interactions lasting 10 minutes or more, and all of the lies they told in those interactions. Most of those lies were unremarkable. People lied, for example, about whether the check was in the mail and whether they cared about where to go for lunch; they feigned liking for people they really didn't like much at all, and overstated how well they had done on a test at school or an assignment at work. When it came to these mostly inconsequential lies, the participants in our studies told relatively few of them to the people in their lives they cared about the most. When nestled in the warmth of a close personal relationship, they set aside the little lies of day to day life for the comforting communications of truths and trust.

When we leave the little light lies behind, however, and venture into the more ominous realm of serious lies, close relationships become treacherous. That is one of the sad lessons of the tale told by Rita. Her experience was hardly unique. The people who told the dupes the most hurtful lies they had ever been told were most often the very people to whom they felt closest. As Warren Jones and his colleagues have noted in their studies of betrayal, "the potential for betrayal by an intimate partner is the 'price' one pays for the benefits of intimacy. In the interpersonal sense, one can be betrayed only by a partner one trusts and with whom one is close, whereas the ultimate protection against betrayal is to have no relationships, or only superficial ones." In our own studies, we found that people not only lie to the ones they love, but also that they often lie *about* love. In both the college student sample and the sample of people from the community, one out of every four participants describing the experience of being duped told about an affair.

Romantic relationships are not the only close relationships fraught with betrayal. Except for best friends, who are rarely implicated in the telling of these most hurtful lies, virtually any close relationship partner will do. Adolescents, for example, often indict their parents for deceiving them most deeply. Still, for both adolescents and married and unmarried adults, it is romantic partners who are most often named. When we sorted the tellers of the serious lies (as named by the dupes) into the categories of romantic partners, parents, siblings, children, other relatives, best friends, friends, acquaintances, and strangers, the romantic partner category bulged with the very disproportionate share of 40 percent of the liars. We seem to save our most important lies for the people with whom we have shared the deepest intimacy, as if those lies were some precious treasure. The dupes, however, rarely see them that way.

Hurts So Bad

When something like this happens, you suddenly have no sense of reality at all. You have lost a piece of your past. The infidelity itself is small potatoes compared to the low-level brain damage that results when a whole chunk of your life turns out to have been completely different from what you thought it was. It becomes impossible to look back at anything that's happened—from the simplest exchange between the two of you at a dinner party to the horrible death of Mr. Abbey—without wondering what was really going on. See the couple. See the couple with the baby. See the couple with the baby having another baby. *What's wrong with this picture?* Everything, as it happens."

--Rachel, from Nora Ephron's *Heartburn*

The most devastating lies are those that obliterate a cherished piece of your identity and your life. When Rita saw the lovely pendant around the neck of the secretary, she learned in that split second that the pendant was not a token of her husband's love for her, but of his devotion to someone else; that her marriage was not "basically happy"; that her husband was not the moral pillar that he seemed; that the life that he had been living with her was a lie; and that the reality that she believed in and lived her life by, was equally fraudulent. One reason why serious lies hurt so bad, then, is that they violently impose a wholesale redefinition of your past, and force you to face a new and uncertain future.

The dupes who seemed to feel most lost, disoriented, and devastated by the discovery of the deceit were those who had been most enmeshed with the persons who betrayed them. As one man noted, "she took up a lot of time and I gave a lot of myself...my mood, my feelings...I guess a lot of my routines were geared around her."

What Kind of Fool Am I?

Dupes were often dutiful, and that hurt, too. Rita spent endless evenings home alone with the kids, with no husband in sight until the wee hours of the morning. She continued uncomplainingly to do his laundry and raise the kids even though he was sometimes cold and uncommunicative for days at a time. She had all her excuses in line ("he has always been a night person", "he is not a warm, outgoing person"). Another woman, Diana, told us of a time when her boyfriend went on a trip to Florida with a few other men, and she decided to surprise him by cleaning his house and buying some new things for it, "just to make it look nice" for him when he got back. Her boyfriend returned before she was finished, and was not expecting to find her there. At his side was his "souvenir of Florida", a seventeen year old girl. The dupes in these cases and many others were acting in good faith, sometimes going even beyond the call of duty to be especially thoughtful and kind. They expected their thoughtfulness to add tenderness to the relationship. Meanwhile, their partner was marinating in someone else's stew.

I was engaged to the girl, and she pulled one over on me.

I felt like a sucker; I felt used.

As these and many other dupes told us so straightforwardly, it hurts to be the target of a serious lie because you feel stupid and foolish. When the relationship with the liar was supposedly a close one ("I was engaged to the girl"), that only adds to the agony. When we counted the kinds of things that our participants said in their stories, we found that one thing the dupes mentioned again and again was that their esteem was hurt by the experience. (The liars, in contrast, hardly ever mentioned in their stories that they had hurt the people they had deceived.) Dupes seemed to feel especially stupid and foolish when the deception had been going on for a long period of time, when they realized in retrospect that there were cues they should have noticed, and when others with far less investment in the episode knew about it before they did.

> "How do you feel?" asked Eve.
> "Hurt. Angry. Stupid. Miserable." I thought for a
> minute. "And dumb."
> "You didn't do this," said Eve. "He did."
> "But I picked him," I said.
>   --Rachel, from Nora Ephron's *Heartburn*

> I always thought I was a pretty shrewd judge of
> character. I thought this was the best thing that ever
> happened to me, and it turned out it was the worst.

We asked our participants to tell us how much they experienced each of a whole list of emotions once they discovered that they had been deceived. The list enumerated by Rachel (from *Heartburn*) was similar to the one that we compiled from the dozens of people who answered our questions. Angry and defiant came out first for both our college students and our participants from the community, followed closely by hurt, depressed, and tense. They were less likely to feel loving or forgiving, and they almost never reported feeling happy or relieved.

In theory, it might make a dupe feel good to lash out at the liars and pronounce them to be slime. It might even feel like especially sweet revenge to register these complaints with a team of psychologists. But there is one big problem

19

with this "I'm okay, you're a slime" reaction: As Rachel points out, it makes you wonder just how okay you really are if you could have picked such a scoundrel. It shakes your faith in your judgment of other people, a faith that for some of our participants, had never before been so challenged.

Both my trust and my love were betrayed.

The dupes sometimes insisted that the lie that was told to them was even worse than the bad behavior that was covered up by the lie. We were curious about this, so we recruited some research assistants who were not party to these lies and who therefore could serve as fairly objective judges, to rate just how hurtful each lie seemed to them, and how hurtful the behaviors seemed that were covered up by the lie. Generally they, too, agreed that the lies seemed even more hurtful than the behaviors they were concealing.

Both the dupes and the research assistants, though, were merely telling us their judgments. They could have been wrong. We don't know whether the people who told us about their experiences would have felt any less badly if, for example, their partner had been completely honest about an affair, while continuing to engage in it. One of our participants did have an experience similar to this. She discovered her husband's affair from hints such as "finding the woman's last name in the back of my husband's shirts from the cleaners, extended overnights away, mysterious calls". Months after being found out, the dupe reports, her husband continues to describe his feelings for his lover. "He still tells of his love for her, her beautiful looks, and dependent ways. He admits that he loves us both, but due to guilt...chooses to stay with me." The "honesty" of her husband's ongoing commentary about his infatuation with his lover seems rather brutal.

What may in fact be especially painful about the discovery of a serious lie, however, is that it is a double whammy. Both the lie and the bad behavior that was covered by the lie are discovered at the same time. Your partner has been having an affair. Your partner has been lying to you. The dupe's misery is compounded.

Life with Liars

How can you have a relationship with someone you don't trust?

Also adding to the misery quotient for dupes is the transformation in their perceptions of the liar. Like Rita, the woman who found that the ordained minister, religion professor, college dean, father of four children, and her husband of almost two decades had actually been spending years in bed with the secretary, most dupes have a new and sullied view of the person who lied to them.

The tellers of serious lies have not only betrayed the dupes, they have also demeaned them. By making a unilateral decision to withhold important information from the dupes, they usurp power and status for themselves, and turn a relationship that may have had some semblance of equality into a monarchy with in which they get to sit on the throne.

The dupes also complained that the experience of being deceived had imposed an emotional distance between themselves and the person who betrayed them. They saw each other less, felt less close to each other, and most importantly, the dupes said they just didn't trust the liar as much anymore. Most of these reactions were strongest immediately after the lie was discovered, but some continued to linger long afterwards.

Draw a New Picture

If we had asked our participants to draw a picture of their personal relationships before they discovered the lie and the infidelity it hid, we think that many of them would have placed themselves and the liar smiling and holding hands in the middle of the page. Their close friends and important relatives would be sketched in nearest to the happy couple, and others would be placed in suitably more distant locations. The discovery of the lie makes a mockery of this pretty picture and forces it to be redrawn. The liars are still at center stage, but their hands are now caressing someone else's. The dupes have been edged out toward the perimeters, where they glare in angrily, and for some, perhaps still longingly.

There is a particularly pernicious variation of this wreck-a-sketch, in which the liar's lover is someone the dupe considered very dear. These are the wrenching double betrayals, in which your partner becomes involved with your sibling, your cousin, or your best friend. The discovery of the lie means the decimation of not one, but two close ties. In the words of one of our participants, "I had a friend, a real friend, and she told me my husband was seeing another woman and I believed her. It turned out she was the other woman and I lost everything including him and her--a friend. How awful."

The Life that Could Have Been

After the initial outrage at the discovery of the lie, the dupes often develop a simmering rage over other injustices. They realize that a part of their life was wrestled from them without their knowledge or consent. Rita eventually found someone else to love her and even speak to her; perhaps she would have preferred to have spent many of the previous years with someone like him, or with friends as her most significant others, instead of staying home with her husband's dirty laundry while he was out vigorously making more of it.

Chapter 2

Deadly Lies

It was about last May and my mom had cancer. And during the time I had an important tennis game and I had been taking SATs too, so everybody in my family knew that she had cancer for three weeks before they told me. And um, my mom tests me a lot, not really tests me, but she asked me different questions. So this one Sunday she came up to me and she said, 'I'm going to the hospital for a week.' And I was like, 'uh, sure.' She was like, 'do you need anything,' and I go, 'no, I just thought you'd give me some money' and stuff like that. I was just kidding around. I didn't think she was serious but then she turned out to have breast cancer. And I never really told anybody but I felt really bad that I wasn't told. You know, they said it was important 'cause I had SATs and they didn't want anything on my mind or anything. And I had the tennis game. They didn't want anything bothering me. But it really did, so I felt like, everybody else in my family knew—all my siblings including even my younger sister. And all during that time, my father had been in a bad mood and me and him had fought a lot 'cause, you know, he was upset about it. I didn't know.

> And that's about it. That's probably the biggest lie. I don't know if it's a lie; maybe they just didn't tell me. That's the biggest one of my life.
>
> --Marty

Twelve percent of the college students and four percent of the people from the community who told us about the most serious lie that was ever told to them, told us stories very much like this one. A person or even a pet to whom they felt deeply attached was seriously ill, dying, or in some instances had already died, and that vital information was withheld from them. Often, the person who withheld the information (or the person to whom the dupes directed most of their anger and resentment about the unshared information) was also someone to whom they felt very close. Parents were the usual culprits, and the dupes lashed out at their mothers even more than their fathers.

This deadly lie, then, illustrates one of the same themes we saw in the lies about sex and love--that usually, the most serious lies that are ever told to us are told by the ones we love. They are the very people who generally refrain from telling us many of the silly little lies of everyday life.

> Sometimes the worst lies are things people
> won't tell you because they want to protect you.

These deadly lies, though, are strikingly different from the love and sex lies in that there is much more ambiguity about the liar's motives. When the liars are hiding their affairs, it seems clear that it is primarily their own necks (and other body parts) that they are out to protect. But when instead the liars are withholding information that they know will be excruciatingly painful for the targets of their lies to hear, a case can be made that they really did have the targets' best interests in mind. For their parts, the dupes may even concede that the liars were concerned about their feelings; but they often disagree with the liars' decision to choose deceit as the way out of the dilemma. The student whose comment about the worst lies is quoted above, also added the following: "Even when people lie to protect other people, or because they think they're doing the right thing, you don't necessarily see it that way." Another noted, "You can't really determine for the person when they are going to grow up and when they're going to have to face things...You should get the chance to face your reactions yourself and not have to have someone decide for you how you're going to react."

27

When liars offer "protection" to dupes by shielding them from the pain of the disclosure, they may see themselves as offering kindness, nurturance, and concern. But the dupes read something else into their offering--a judgment on their maturity and their ability to cope. To them, a protective gesture can be a condemnation of them as fragile, immature, and emotionally vulnerable. These are hot issues for adolescents. It seems altogether appropriate that most of the lies of this nature were described by our college student participants as they looked back on their experiences growing up.

More Missed Opportunities

> I never told him what he meant to me, and I never thanked him for all the things he did for me.

When people are deceived about their partners' affairs, their opportunity to reinvest in a more fulfilling life is unwittingly postponed until the infidelity is uncovered. In the instances of deadly lies, the opportunities are not just postponed, they are obliterated. The young woman quoted above was discussing her favorite uncle, the one who showered her with affection and granted her every wish. She never got to thank him. Another woman told of going to summer camp while her grandmother was hospitalized. Her mother encouraged her to write to her grandmother, but repeatedly insisted that her grandmother would be fine. Feeling reassured, the woman never did write to her grandmother. By the time she got home from camp, her grandmother was dead.

Such missed opportunities are only the most obvious ones. There are others as well. Marty, the young man quoted at the opening of this section who was the last to learn of his mother's cancer, missed out on the opportunity to be a part of the emotional bonding that sometimes transpires within a family in the midst of a crisis. He also missed out on opportunities to provide support to his mom, tolerance to his dad, and nurturance to his sisters. And he missed the opportunity to cope in tandem with his loved ones; by the time he was let in on the news, the others around him had already had weeks to process emotionally the significance of the events that were unfolding.

Telling Secrets and Spreading the Word: The Pecking Order

But when I really found out the truth and found out that a bunch of other people knew, then it really hurt.

The famous anthropologist Edward Sapir once said that nonverbal communication occurs "in accordance with an elaborate and secret code that is written nowhere, known to none, and understood by all." I think there is a similar code, at least in certain Western cultures, that governs the verbal communication of important information. The code is a pecking order, and it dictates who should tell what to whom, and in what order. When Marty expressed his chagrin that "even [his] younger sister" knew before he did that his mom had cancer, my colleagues and I immediately understood why this was so hurtful to him. This was not because of any inside knowledge we had gained as researchers; we expect that anyone reading his account would feel the same. In his status as an older sibling, he felt that he had a right to know deeply significant family news no later than his younger sibling, and that the other family members had a complementary obligation to tell him. The violation of these rules of disclosure on such a weighty matter predictably causes resentment and pain.

The pecking order theme was also prominent in the lies about sex and love. One young woman described her boyfriend Bill's affair with another woman. The dupe's best friends were Mary (Bill's cousin) and Lynn. The person who was betrayed told us that soon after discovering the infidelity, "I was talking to Lynn and I go, 'Wait, do you know about this?' For some reason, it just occurred to me that Bill could have told Mary and Mary could have told Lynn. And they were supposed to be my two best friends and so they knew the whole time and they never told me. And I was really mad. It was really upsetting because I felt like such a fool....So that really kinda blew my friendship with my friends. I was really mad at them for a long time...And then we just grew away from each other and they just became best friends and I started hanging around with different friends. And so the whole thing was just really awful."

The dupe's implicit knowledge of the rules of disclosure led her to her accurate suspicions. Of course Bill would tell Mary, because they were cousins. And then of course Mary would tell Lynn because they were friends. And then Mary and Lynn would tell the dupe because they were her two best friends. But wait, they never told her! And they knew the entire time. The consequences for the friendship alliances were profound. Mary and Lynn shared a secret and kept it from their friend; ultimately, they became best friends and the dupe was pushed completely out of the picture. Another sketch wrecked.

Other Deadly Lies

The lies involving the withholding of news of a grave illness or impending death comprised the biggest subcategory of the "death, illness, and violence" grouping, but there were others as well. There were lies about child sexual abuse, spousal violence, a miscarriage, and herpes. There were also stories in which the liars falsely claimed to be pregnant, to have been raped, and to have cancer. But perhaps the lie most deserving of the "deadly" label is the following: "During the war, my commanding officer instructed me to move my platoon through a village he knew to be heavily defended. He told me there were no enemy in the area. As a result, we entered the village unprepared for combat. Three of my men were killed and two wounded."

Chapter 3

Lies That Are a Matter of Honor

I always wanted an animal to pet when I was little. But my mom doesn't like animals, so all we got was goldfish. Finally, when I was 10, my mother broke down when we saw these cute little kittens and we got one and took her home and named her Fluffy. And we just loved Fluffy and she was such a smart cat and she was just so pretty. And we had her for about three years and then we had to go away for a year for my dad's work so we couldn't take Fluffy with us. So we gave her to a neighbor for a year. It was kind of hard not to see Fluffy but it was just for a year. So we went away and about the middle of the year we got a phone call from the neighbor that Fluffy had run away and I remember crying. I was really attached to that cat and me and my sister Mandy were really upset. To comfort us our parents said, 'Oh don't worry, you know we will get you another cat; as a matter of fact, we will get you a dog.' I mean wow, a dog and I mean dogs actually communicate with you. And so that kind of quieted us down. And so when the year was out and we got back home and we said,

> 'OK, dad, it's time to get the dog." And my mom said, 'No way are we having a dog in this house.' And that really upset me. They used the promise to quiet us down and that really got us mad. And I remember being on a rampage for two years, having a sheep dog fund and begging my mother about once a week. I remember always being a little bit mad at my parents. Even now I might bring up how I can't always trust them because of what they did to me.
>
> —Stephen

We seldom enter into formal contractual arrangements with the ones we love. A promise about a serious matter is almost by definition a *solemn* promise. When the person making the promise says or implies, "You have my word for it", what is exchanged is a matter of honor. The promisers can offer only their word to people they feel close to because their word is backed by their honor; and the people to whom promises are made honor the promisers' word by asking for nothing more. When such a promise is broken, it is the promiser's honor that is damaged. The discredited promise-makers who try to offer another promise to the same targets may find that their word is regarded as counterfeit currency, no longer backed by the solid gold of their honor.

The parents in the tale of Fluffy and the dog were faced with their children's deep distress. They dealt with that by promising not just to get them a new cat but to top that and buy them an even more coveted pet--a dog. Their hope, as Stephen explained later in the interview, was that their kids would be immediately comforted, and that in the subsequent six months of their time away, would gradually forget about the dog. Instead, their joyful anticipation continued to swell. When at last the no-dog dictum became definitive, it was a very big bubble of hope that had been burst.

Stephen admits to being relentless in taunting his parents about their breach of faith. He spearheads a campaign against them, with his sheep dog fund and his weekly pleadings. Years later, he still gets in his digs. He is probably chiding them not just for breaking their promise, but also for taking the coward's way out by making the promise in the first place. Also, like some of the other dupes who described stories in which the news of the death or serious illness of a loved one was withheld from them, Stephen probably also felt deeply offended by the implication that he was not mature enough to handle the truth.

When we asked the people who were deceived a series of standard questions about why the liars lied to them, we expected them to say that the liars lied for selfish reasons--for example, to make themselves look or feel better. The dupes, and even the liars themselves, did sometimes say this, but it was not their number one reason. The reason most strongly endorsed by both the dupes and the liars was keeping the peace: They all thought that the liars lied first and foremost to avoid tension, conflict, and embarrassment. Lies such as this one often succeed grandly at restoring the peace. But if and when they are discovered, the war that erupts can far surpass in longevity, intensity, and bitterness the initial battle that the lies were meant to squelch.

The story of Fluffy and the dog also illustrates the emotions experienced most frequently and most intensely by the dupes. Their very strongest emotional reactions to the lie were anger and defiance. The cluster of pained reactions--feeling hurt, depressed, and tense--was almost as severe. The liars hoped that their lies would keep the tension, conflict, and intense negativity at bay; instead, once the lies were discovered, these very reactions exploded in their face.

Chapter 4

Whose Flesh and Blood?
Lies About Kinship

When I was a small child, I don't even remember what it was about, but my sister and I were having a disagreement and she hit me. My mother was going to spank her and she ran away screaming, "She's not my sister anyway. She belongs to old Billy Joe." From that day on, I was never sure of myself. But as I grew up, the older I got, the more I looked like my father's mother. Today I look more like her than any of her children, so I have to believe she did this to hurt me because she was mad. I never knew where she got such an idea. But I always looked for signs of any way I looked like my father. I took care of him until he died. One morning while I was sitting on the bed beside him holding him so he wouldn't fall over, I was looking down at his feet. I remember thinking that my feet look like his. I'm sure as long as I live I will never forget and I can still see her saying those awful words that made me have doubts about myself.

--Betty

Whose child am I? It is hard to think of a more deeply personal question or a question more central to a person's identity and sense of self than this one. At age 75, this woman described to us a taunt hurled at her by her sister when she was eight years old that continued to haunt her for the next six or seven decades of her life. We take seriously her prediction that she will never forget it. This was perhaps the most lingering of all of the lies that were described to us. For years and years, this woman scrutinized the faces and even the feet of would-be relatives for signs of authentic kinship. It is an agonizing search for truth because she will never find the perfectly definitive sign.

What is fascinating about this lie is the possibility it raises about the liar. We never interviewed the liar and so we cannot know for sure what her motives actually were, but it is entirely possible that her remark was simply a childish jibe utterly lacking in truth value, motivated solely by momentary fear, frustration, and anger. If we did interview that woman, she may well say that she has no memory whatsoever of this incident that was permanently imprinted upon her sister's psyche. In fact, she may have forgotten it almost as soon as she said it.

Chapter 5

Lies About Fortune and Livelihood

This lie was told to me many years ago, but I still remember it as the most deliberate lie anyone has ever told me. Maybe there have been others, but if so, I was not aware of the fact.

My husband and I celebrate our 33rd wedding anniversary this month. It was he who told me the most unforgettable lie that I can recall. He is really not known as a liar, BUT he told me this one!

We were both working when we married in 1956. Though we both had good jobs at the time, salaries back then weren't too big. A large portion of our salaries went for rent, so we decided to save in order to buy a house. After about three years our nest egg had grown--to no huge, sizeable amount, but enough for a down-payment on a house.

It was about now that a friend of his (who was dabbling in the stock market) got my husband interested in buying shares in a new-found company overseas. We discussed the issue and I finally said that I didn't think we should. I did ask several times if he had bought shares. "No," was the standard answer I got.

A couple, maybe several, months passed before the check that he had written cleared the bank. This is how I found out about it. We had a joint checking account, and when the cancelled checks came through, I saw what he had done!

So many years have passed that it is hard to recall all of the emotions that I felt! But I remember that I was shocked, mad, hurt, and flabbergasted! I really can't remember all his excuses—I'm sure it was hope to 'get rich quick.' Needless to say, we never earned a dime on the deal. The company folded. And when the time came for us to buy our first house?!? You guessed it! We borrowed the money!

--Rosemarie

The themes illustrated by Rosemarie's lie are by now quite familiar ones. The lie was told by the person Rosemarie probably felt closer to than anyone else in her life. It was the person she would picture herself with, holding hands, in the center of the drawing. Wreck-a-sketch. Redraw the picture. Her husband joins forces with a buddy, and she is unknowingly pushed aside. Her reactions are exactly the ones we have seen over and over again, and in exactly the order that we most often see them--she was furious, and she was hurt.

Establishing financial and emotional independence, acquiring one's very own home...these are among the central life tasks of couples who are just beginning to build their life together. Time and again, we found that when dupes pointed to the most serious lie that had ever been told to them, they were pointing to a place where, at that time in their lives, they had invested their heart and soul.

PART 2

Deeper into Deceit

Chapter 6

The Why and How of Serious Lies, and What Happens Afterwards

But Why?

> I think this person lied to me because he was self-centered. He only cared about himself and he only wanted to fill his own desires. He really didn't care about anybody else but himself. And he had to lie just so I would pay attention to him and do what he said because otherwise if he told me the truth, I wouldn't have done anything he told me to.

After hearing so many stories filled with pain and woe, the answer just quoted is about what we expected from the targets of lies when asked directly why they thought the liar had lied to them. We expected them to say that the liars lied because they were self-serving, self-centered scoundrels. And in fact, in almost a third of the dupes' responses to the question about the liar's motives, there was some derogation of the liars as self-centered. What was more surprising, however, was how rarely the targets merely left their answers at that.

> He lied to me probably because he was embarrassed about the fact that he had given me herpes and he felt bad about it. And probably because he didn't want to hurt me.

> I think she lied to me because I think she really did like me and I don't think she wanted me to know that she had accepted a dinner engagement with another guy.

The first of the quotes is from a woman who contracted herpes from the first man she ever slept with. When she called him with her medical evidence (and her own knowledge of the impossibility of having contracted it from anyone else), he said it was news to him. Still, she claims that he lied so as not to hurt her.

The second quote is from a man whose girlfriend broke a dinner date with him with the excuse that her grandparents were visiting and she was staying home with them. He decides to go out to dinner with a buddy, and when he arrives at the restaurant, notices a guy sitting alone at a table set with a mysteriously quivering tablecloth. Eventually, his girlfriend comes out from under the table, the tablecloth lies still, and the deception is revealed. Still, he insists that she lied to him because "she really did like me".

Other targets said that the liars lied because they were concerned about how the targets might react if they told the truth. According to the dupes, the liars were worried that the dupes might respect them less, or might not understand their point of view, or might be angry, or might not approve of their actions.

Dupes made other excuses for the liars, too:

- "He didn't mean to lie. It just started out as a joke."
- "I think he was really confused about what he wanted."
- "She probably lied just because she didn't know what else to do."

Some of the dupes said that the liars lied because they felt so ashamed or so embarrassed about what they had done, or because they were such troubled (insecure, scared, lonely, jealous) souls. As one young woman said: "I guess she lied because she was scared of losing her best friend and scared of being alone."

Dupes also thought liars lied because it was so important to them to control the knobs of the wreck-a-sketch. They wanted to control other people's emotions (especially their jealousy and their affection) and their emotional alliances. Often, this occurred in the context of romance, when, for example, a liar tried to pit two lovers against each other so she could step in and woo the disenchanted man. But it occurred in nonromantic alliances, too, as when a high school girl claimed to have been raped to rekindle the interests of two friends who were becoming closer to each other than to her. In these instances, too, the dupes sometimes seem surprisingly understanding when discussing the liars' motives. The person who was fooled by the faked claim of rape, for example, explained, "She lied because she felt left out...And she wanted to have something big, so that we'd think of her. She just wanted to get our attention again."

About one out of every three targets, in response to the question of why the liar told the lie, claimed that the liar had the targets' best interests at heart--they wanted to protect them, comfort them, tell them what they wanted to hear, or spare them from the pain of being hurt or worried or upset. When the lie involved the withholding of news about the death or serious illness of a loved one, this "protectiveness" motive was mentioned almost 90% of the time.

Why were the dupes so charitable in their interpretations of the liars' motives? The role of the dupe is not an enviable one. They have been suckered and hurt. Moreover, when they were suckered and hurt by someone with whom they were romantically involved, as was so often the case, the pain was inflicted by someone they had chosen as their relationship partner. One way to salvage their esteem was to insist that the liars really did have their best interests at heart, or that they wanted to preserve the relationship, or that they were just lonely or confused. Maybe their indulgence also helps them to reinvest in the relationship, or to move on to other relationships or to other passions in their lives, with some of their faith and trust still intact.

The How of Lying:
How Serious Lies Are Discovered

Some deeply serious lies never are discovered. Those stories can come only from the lie-tellers. When dupes describe their experiences as targets, they are, of course, talking about lies that they have discovered. As Betty's story indicates, though, there can be an element of lingering doubt about whether a lie really was told even in the dupes' stories.

We were interested in learning how targets went about trying to uncover deceit once they became suspicious, and how they thought the liars had schemed to cover their tracks. Some dupes, though, were so totally taken by the deceit that they never did become suspicious, and so of course they never used any particular lie-detection strategies. The liars, in turn, were never challenged with accusations or recriminations, and so they had little plotting or planning to do to ensure the successful perpetration of their deceits. In addition to these clueless dupes, there were also targets who told us that they simply did not want to know the truth and so they made no effort to discover it. My suspicion about these people is that at some level, they already knew.

Lie Upon Lie

Among those dupes who have their suspicions and do not try to run away from them, their favorite strategy is to confront the liars directly. As far as they can tell, the liars' favorite ploy in response to their accusations is to deny them and perhaps tell a few more lies. The targets' second favorite strategy for uncovering the lie is to ask other people what they know; the liars' second favorite strategy for keeping the lie hidden (at least according to the dupes' views) is to ask other people not to tell what they know. Next, dupes say that they scrutinize the liars' behaviors, mannerisms, and nonverbal behaviors. In turn, they think that the liars try to avoid relevant topics and to respond evasively to those risky topics that do come up.

How, then, does the truth finally break through? Most commonly, it is a third person who reveals it, either on their own initiative or in response to the dupe's inquiries. The story I will use to illustrate this comes not from one of the participants in my research but from my mother. When she was a teenager, her mother was in and out of the hospital for treatments for cancer. My mother knew that her mother was very ill, but not that she was dying. She learned the truth when walking home from school one day with a friend, who said to her, "You know, your mother is never going to get well."

The second most common path to the truth is the smoking gun. A pendant tellingly adorns the secretary's neck; a check for a risky investment clears the bank. A life is forever changed.

Perhaps it is true, as Catholics would have us believe, that confession is good for the soul. Liars, though, seem to seek their salvation in other ways. In the stories that the dupes told us, only about one in five of the liars fessed up to their lies.

The most interesting mode of discovery psychologically is the one that occurs only very gradually over time, as the deceived person grows older and wiser, and looks back upon the deceptive episode in a deeper and more insightful way each time. In these examples, it is difficult for the dupes to point to one particular moment when they finally knew for sure that they had been deceived; instead, they describe more of a subtly developing awareness: "It's hard for me to remember exactly when I discovered it. As you grow older, you know, you put things together...like you know that couldn't have been true."

Among the most dramatic discoveries are those in which the liars are caught red-handed (or, more typically, bare-bottomed). The classic example in the media is of course the dupe who finds his or her spouse in bed with another person. We did hear a few such tales from our participants, as well as several variations (for example, the dupe decides to go to the liar's apartment to confront him with her suspicions about his infidelity, and he appears at the door zipping his fly). This mode of discovery, though, was the most infrequent of them all.

How Does It Feel?
Emotional Hide and Seek

When targets told us about their reactions to discovering the lies, they said that they felt deeply angered and hurt, and that they showed it. But most of the time, they claimed, what they showed was just a muted version of what they really felt. The son who tormented his parents about their broken promise to replace Fluffy with a dog was an exception to the rule that dupes try to hide some of their feelings instead of dramatizing them.

Dupes tried to hide how badly they were feeling not only at the moment when they discovered the lie, but also in their subsequent encounters with the liar and with the rest of the world. Some were suppressing before they even realized they were being deceived. These attempts at hiding their feelings were hard work, and they made the dupes feel anxious and lonely.

We asked a young man whose girlfriend claimed to be pregnant how he felt during the time that she was deceiving him, as he made the arrangements to "have everything taken care of". He replied, "This is something I couldn't share with anyone. I kept it all bottled up within myself like a Coke can that had been shaken up and I was very very unhappy."

Another woman told a story about one of her best friends who told her that "nothing was wrong" when she had to go into the hospital. Eventually, the target learned that her friend had actually had a miscarriage, and had told other friends and even the dupe's parents and still never admitted it to the dupe until she found out from someone else. The woman who was deceived told us about how difficult it was for her when she saw her friend after that: "I tried to be nice to her on the outside, but I was really quite hurt on the inside."

Finally, a young man described a harrowing family story that happened while he was at a friend's house. Back home, his father pulled a gun on his mother and sister, the police were called, and he was put in jail. Later that evening when he was released, he told his son that he hadn't done anything and had simply been set up.

The target told us about his interactions with other people after this horrifying event. "I was sort of to myself. Felt sort of different from other people. So lonely. But my mood, I'd be angry. Real angry. But I'd never show it. I'd be real sad, but I'd never show it. I could be very depressed, but I'd never show it. So, I was sort of like on both sides, putting on an act. I was acting to the public to make everything seem like it was going smooth when inside I was fighting with myself."

Happy Endings

Although serious lies are often devastating to the dupes in the short run, they are not inevitably horrendous in the long run. Sometimes the lie changes the deceived person's life, and in a way that the person sees as immeasurably better. Rita's story is again a good example. Her pious husband had been cheating on her for years, but eventually she left him, and her life story took a rewarding turn: "Today I'm a very happy lady, married for three years to a wonderful guy who is my closest friend as well as husband."

For other dupes, what changed was not so much some concrete circumstance of their life, but rather their understanding of themselves, of others, and of the world. They took from their otherwise painful experience an important life lesson.

For targets who described lies from their childhood or adolescence, often what their eyes were opened to were the clay feet of the gods. One person described how in grade school he was tricked into confessing to writing on the bathroom walls by a nun (who was the principal) who claimed to have brought in a handwriting expert who matched the writing to the dupe's. When we asked him about the long-term consequences of the lie, he said, "You know, being brought up in a Catholic family, going to a Catholic school, having to listen to nuns from first through eighth grade and all through high school, it kind of shocks you the first time you come to realize these people are not just human but they actually can do things sly and underhanded such as this...it changed my whole perspective on nuns and authority..."

More commonly, it is the children's and adolescents' parents who get knocked off the pedestal by their lies. One of the college men whose parents lied to him about the grave illness of his grandfather (by saying he was only in the hospital for tests and would be fine) had this to say in response to our question of how the lie changed his relationship with the liars: "I was made more aware of the fact that my parents were capable of lying...I guess, overall, I was better able to understand my parents as people..."

Sometimes the lessons that dupes described were not specific to any particular people or even categories of people, but were more like general life lessons. What is the "life lesson" learned from hearing your father call you from jail and then deny that he had just pulled a gun on your mother and sisters and threatened to kill them?: "I think it made me grow up to the world...I learned to cope with life and people everyday in a better way. You know, there weren't too many things people could say to me, or anything that could happen to me, that would get me real down that I couldn't put myself back up. This incident gave me strength. Mental strength. Keep on going."

Finally, a young man whose mother had hid from him for years the fact that his father had serious psychological problems offered this observation about how the experience changed his life: "It made me think about all the times I've lied to people and how it can hurt them by not telling the truth and how important it is to tell the truth." What was so remarkable about this young man's reflections is that they were so utterly nondefensive. Unlike virtually every other dupe who insisted that it was <u>the liar</u> who had done wrong and needed to reform, this person cast his moral glance inward and resolved to be a better person himself.

The Dupe Role Revisited: Poor Me

If I had to summarize the tales of the dupes in two words, those words would be "poor me". Dupes feel that they have been wronged, and they seem not at all reluctant to say so. Some even elaborate the "poor me" theme by enumerating other life burdens. For example, the wife of the pilot who was enamored of the flight attendant's "beautiful looks and dependent ways" opened her own sad saga like this: "Background information on me during the 2 year span was the following: 1, My husband allowed us to move back to Richmond to let me take care of a 70 year old mother and father dying a terrible death with cancer. 2, My husband's schedule allowed him home only 10 days a month with his home base three hours away. 3, We 'put down' my devoted 14 year old dog." A woman who discovered her husband's plans to leave her after he was murdered on the way to the airport appended her life tragedies to the end of her tale: "...my home burned to the ground two months after my husband died; two car accidents involving my daughter; just this month, a broken leg from being kicked by a horse, the sad and tragic death of her horse, her two dogs stolen at night, and this week a lump in her breast..."

So far, I have accepted the dupes' accounts at face value. Surely, some of them were innocent victims of unspeakable cruelty. But there are, I suspect, other dimensions to their experience as well.

The "Warm Bath of Innocent Victimization"

The truth is that I was secretly pleased when she slept with Charlie because I was exonerated from the guilt of all those years of feeling jealous of her and was plunged suddenly into a warm bath of innocent victimization.

That's the catch about betrayal, of course: that it feels good, that there's something immensely pleasurable about moving from a complicated relationship which involves minor atrocities on both sides to a nice, neat, simple one where one person has done something so horrible and unforgivable that the other person is immediately absolved of all the low-grade sins of sloth, envy, gluttony, avarice and I forget the other three.

--Rachel, in Nora Ephron's *Heartburn*

The dupes who told us their tales were very adept at the victim role. They not only wallowed in the warm bath of victimization; they got their listeners to wallow with them. The college students we interviewed each told us about two experiences, one in which they were the dupe and one in which they were the liar. We recruited people who were not involved in any of the lies to listen to the audio recordings of these interviews of the many different students describing their two different lies. They listened to them in mixed up orders, such that they did not hear the same person's two stories in a row. In fact, they were not even told that they might listen to the same person more than once. After each of the many stories they heard, we asked them several questions, including how much they liked the person who told the story and how physically attractive they imagined the person to be. After hearing the students tell their stories about being betrayed, victimized, and duped, the listeners liked the students better, and thought they were more attractive, than when they listened to the exact same students telling their stories about when they had lied to someone else. In taking the role of the victim, the dupes seemed to be able to elicit the empathy and even the affection of their listeners.

Like Rachel, some of our dupes articulated their feeling that being victimized by the liar gave them emotional absolution for their own sins-- sometimes even the same kinds of sins for which they were now condemning the liar. As one woman put it, "...when I found out about the lie, it made me feel better because I had deceived him a little bit too and so it made me feel like, 'Well, fine, I don't have to feel guilty about that because he did the same to me.'" What this woman has revealed, though, is that she was not totally innocent after all.

Her story was among the clearest on this point. But many others were suggestive.

Underwear in a *Briefcase*?

The opening story of the wife of the religion professor at first blush appears to be the tale of a totally innocent and unsuspecting victim. And my best guess is that it really is. But there is something that bothers me about that reading of the story: Why was she looking for his dirty underwear in his briefcase? Was she really wholly unsuspicious? And if not, did the suspicion grow only in response to the fishy behavior of the liar, or did the relationship have a modicum of distrust even before any flagrant violations of intimacy occurred?

In other stories, it is not just one relationship, but a whole family of them, that seems to be infused with suspicion and distrust. People's eyes and hands wander into private places that are not their own. One such example comes from a student who talked about his parents' divorce. After his mom and dad announced the news, he asked them both individually whether they had ever had an affair. Both parents denied it. Here's his report of his subsequent discovery: "...about six months later, I found this piece of paper in my mother's drawer that was a list of all these women that my father had had affairs with..." It was then apparent that his father had lied to him. Of course, his father had also lied to his mother. And his mother had withheld from him an important reason for the divorce. And he had his hands in his mother's drawer. And his mother had hired a detective to spy on his father. There are victims in this story, and the dupe does appear to be one of them. But this seems to be a family in which victims also double as perpetrators and sneaks, and it is not clear whether their own snooping and sleazing is merely a response to the victimization or if it had an earlier life of its own. Just as some families have traditions of hanging stockings on the night before Christmas and sending amusing cards on birthdays, others might have the traditions of prying and lying.

Dupes Who Push the Liars to Lie

It happened one weekend when I was playing football with my high school team. It was a very difficult game and trying weekend. I was very happy to come home to my girlfriend, tell her about my good experiences and ask her about how her weekend had gone. She told me she had just gone shopping and then gone to the movies that night with some friends. One of my best friends was in the room with me at the time and I hung up and was telling him about what she had told me. My friend looked at me in an odd way and said, "There's no way! She was at a party that night. She came with a bunch of guys." I looked at him. I didn't believe him. I cussed him out. He had to be lying to me.

There is no possible way that Sharlene, my girlfriend, could deceive me in any sort of way. I started to shake. Never, never, had she even come close to deceiving. I wondered if she'd maybe lied to me before. Well, I called her up and I was quite, quite angry. I really shouldn't have been that much. The main reason she lied to me is 'cause she was afraid I'd be angry. I tried to explain to her that I was even more angry because she tried to deceive me... What were the long term consequences of the lie? I was suspicious from then on that she might not have enough faith in me or enough trust in me to go ahead and tell me everything she was doing. On the other hand, it made me realize that I can't force her into a situation where she must lie to me.

No other dupe was as insightful (or as forthcoming) as this young man about his own role in provoking another person to tell him a serious lie. His own behavior and temperament was critical in pulling the lie out of his girlfriend. He was a hothead and he knew it. He cussed out his good buddy and he berated his girlfriend. What was remarkable was his realization that his anger essentially pushed his girlfriend to lie to him, and that if he wanted her to be more honest with him, he would have to change his *own* behavior.

Intimidation by anger was not even the most compelling form of emotional blackmail that we found in the dupe's reports. Diana, the woman who told of tidying up her boyfriend's apartment to sweeten his return from Florida, only to have him show up with his 17-year old "souvenir", went on to describe a whole series of feints and ruses her boyfriend used as he tried to decide whether to fess up or to continue to lie. When at last he and his new friend came to Diana's place to have a serious talk with her, she ran into the bathroom, slit both wrists, and cried for help. Her dramatic gesture was an expression of her pain. But it was also a powerful threat which made it hard for him to cheat on her again, and even harder to tell the truth about it if he did.

Some of your emotions will make you want to believe.

The hothead and the wrist-slitter forced their romantic partners to lie to them by making it so hard for them to tell the truth. Other targets simply made it easy for others to lie. Whether knowingly, unknowingly, or (more likely) semi-knowingly, dupes sometimes collude in the telling of the lies. Sometimes they told us this themselves, fairly explicitly:
- "I really wanted to believe him."
- "I didn't really use any strategies [for detecting the lie] because I really didn't want to know...I basically let myself believe whatever I wanted to."
- "I hoped he was right."

In other examples, the dupes in their loudest voices complain insistently about being deceived, but they can't quite silence their little whispers of collusion. In the story told by Marty, the high school student whose family withheld the news of his mother's cancer, you can hear the whisper when he acknowledges that his mother did tell him that she was going to the hospital. His reply? "Uh, sure." She tries again, asking if he needs anything. He still won't bite: "No, I just thought you'd give me some money." He defends his response by saying that he thought she was just kidding. I think he joined his entire family in perpetrating this lie. He was both the deceiver and the deceived.

PART 3

Stories from the Liars

1. The Most Primitive Lie: Avoiding Punishment and Blame *(Chapter 7)*

2. Entitlement Lies: Lying for What You Think You Deserve *(Chapter 8)*

3. Instrumental Lies *(Chapter 9)*

4. Lies About Passions *(Chapter 10)*

5. Identity Lies: Becoming a Different Person *(Chapter 11)*

6. Taking a Fall: Lies Told to Cover for Someone Else *(Chapter 12)*

7. Living a Lie *(Chapter 13)*

When we asked the participants in our research to tell us about the most serious lies they had ever told to anyone else, what was most striking was how different their tales were from those told by the dupes. The categories of lies that emerged from the liars and from the targets of the lies hardly overlapped at all. For example, not a single liar from among the college students or the people from the community described a time when they had withheld or denied the news of the death or serious illness of a loved one. Instead, if the topic of death appeared among the liars' tales, it was more likely to be in the form of that favorite student excuse, "I couldn't take the test because my grandfather died." (One student in our research who used this excuse found his creative excuse-making skills greatly challenged when, two weeks later, his grandfather really did die.) Nor did the liars describe lies about kinship (the "whose child am I?" kind of lie). Even when the liars did relate stories about the same kind of lie that the dupes described, they told fewer such stories and (as we will see) they told them in an entirely different tone. For instance, whereas one out of every four of the people who were deceived described lies about affairs, only about one in ten of our liars described infidelities that they had committed.

The lies described by the liars fell into seven major categories. Here are some of their stories.

Chapter 7

The Most Primitive Lie:
Avoiding Punishment and Blame

I was in ninth or tenth grade and we were living in South Carolina in this really big southern belle house and my mom had this really old station wagon that just sat in the driveway most of the time. One day it was my turn to cut the side yard and the driveway is really close to that part of the grass. So my dad told me to make sure I cut it around that side because if I didn't it was going to be so hard to cut next time. I couldn't get by there with the lawn mower because the station wagon was in the way. And I knew that if I waited until my parents got home to move the car it would be dark and late. I wouldn't have time to wash my hair and get dressed and ready and I'd probably be so tired from just sitting around waiting for them that I wouldn't want to go out anyway. And so I decided that I was going to move the station wagon and I was like 14 at the time and I didn't have a driver's license or anything and I'd never driven a car before. I started it up and the engine sounded really loud and so I put my foot on one of the pedals and I pulled the little gear shifter down and the car jerked forward so I put my foot down. I thought I was putting it on the brake but I put it on the gas instead. So like I put my foot on the gas really hard to try to stop the car before it went anywhere and it floored the car. It went through the garage door, into the first floor of the house, and ended up against the couch. I was like, "I don't believe this shit." All the neighbors came running around. And when my parents came home, they saw this big hole in the side of the house and they didn't know what had happened. I knew I couldn't tell my dad that I didn't know how to drive a car and I just didn't want to wait for him to come home because that sounds so stupid, he'd be so pissed, and I'd have been punished and everything for quite a long time. So I told him I was trying to finish cutting the grass before it got dark because he wanted me to cut it that day, and I couldn't find any neighbors to help me move the car so I just started it and it jumped forward and it jumped out of gear and ran through the garage. And my dad and mom believed it because my mom said well, yeah, it does have a kind of jump start and it does jerk because it's a really old car. There was a lot of damage to the house but the insurance company paid for it because my mom lied and said she was the one driving the car.

—Terry

When the participants in our research answered our question about the most serious lie they ever told to anyone, they more often told us about a mishap involving a car than about cheating on a romantic partner. In contrast, not a single dupe said that the most serious lie anyone ever told to them had anything to do with such things. The dupes' stories were about people, relationships, emotions, and alliances--not about cars.

A guilty conscience is better than a sore behind.

When you are younger, you always worry more about the consequences than about the fact that it is morally wrong to lie.

Lies told to avoid punishment and blame are the most primitive of all lies. They are usually a child's first lie, and the kind of lie told most frequently for many years. Often, lies told to avoid punishment are construed as children's lies. We know that adults, too, lie to avoid punishment and blame, but somehow we expect relatively more of their lies to be borne of more complex and sophisticated blends of motives and desires. When the *dupes* talked about the motives they saw in the kinds of lies that they described, they sometimes listed motive after motive--e.g., "He lied so I wouldn't worry about him; because he knew I wouldn't approve; because I would tell him to go to England before he wanted to; to make himself look more stable." Yet when we looked at the *liars'* stories and tallied them by motive, we found that the biggest category was the one consisting of these primitive lies about misdeeds told primarily to avoid punishment and pain.

The liars' stories were similar to the dupes' in that in the majority of them, the other party to the lie was someone close to them. But whereas the dupes most often described lies told to them by romantic partners, the liars were relatively more likely to have told their lies to their parents. In their focus on fear of punishment, the liars often described lies they told to people who had the authority to punish them--parents and others of higher status than themselves. The targets of lies, in contrast, were more likely to describe lies told to them by people whose primary power over them was emotional. They were people who were more likely to hurt their feelings than their behinds-- often, people of approximately equal status as themselves.

If you look back on it, it's funny. But it was serious. If I had killed my sister or something, there could have been a lot of problems, and I didn't think about that when I got in the car. I just sort of got in, and then tried to lie my way out of it to keep myself from getting into trouble.

Primitive lies are often careless lies told to cover careless misdeeds. Commonly, the liars did not intend or want the bad behavior to happen. Sometimes they could have anticipated the possible ill effects if they really thought about them, but they didn't bother to do so. The tellers of primitive lies live in the present. They just do something stupid, something bad follows, and then they lie to try to cover their stupidity and their bad deed. Because they didn't plan on trouble, they didn't also didn't plan a lie to get them out of trouble. Although Linda, the young woman in this story, still managed to concoct a good one, other tellers of primitive lies made up some of the worst lies we have ever heard.

> At first I was going to try to pin it on my sister, 'cause she was like four years younger than me. Well, she couldn't even reach the gas and the steering wheel at the same time, so that didn't work. So I just had to say that it was the car's fault. Anything but me. I just couldn't deal with that.

Poor little siblings--they are easy targets for blame. Terry resisted the temptation, but apparently only because of the implausibility of the resulting story, and not because of any moral pangs. Other liars could fit their younger sibs into a more seamless story, and some of them went ahead and did so.

What is more important about Terry's comment than her litany of possible targets for blame is her realization that she had to blame someone or something in order to spare her own psyche. This is what makes lies so tempting, and the truth so hard to tell: In telling the truth in instances like these, you are acknowledging something about yourself that you don't want anyone else to know--something you would rather not even know yourself.

All in the Family

The young woman who drove the family car into the living room was not the only liar in her family. Terry's mother lied to the insurance company, and her father was at least a silent accomplice in getting the insurance company to pay a huge sum of money for repairs to a garage, a living room, and a station wagon. Perhaps children learn lying by example, and one surmises that Terry had many such examples when she was growing up.

Later in the interview, Terry told us how she got caught. The day she got her permit, her mother told her to put the car in reverse and she didn't know how. Her mother's reaction?: "Well, damn, you just lied back then, didn't you? I used to lie when I was little, too, but I never got caught like you do. You just can't lie as good as we used to in the old days." This was a very unusual parental response to the discovery of a child's lie. Lying, this mother seemed to imply, was a sport, a competition in which the most skilled athlete wins. Her daughter just wasn't as good an athlete as she was in her youth. All told, this may have been a very lie-indulgent family.

The next example of a primitive lie illustrates a very different family dynamic and a very different set of feelings about the lie-telling episode.

I guess it was when I was in about fifth grade and my sister was dating a boy at a the University of Oklahoma. I was pretty little and my big deal was I wanted to know what girls and boys would talk about on the telephone. I just didn't understand. This boy would call her and I'd get real curious. And our family is really, really based on trust. I mean, we're really conscious about how no one lies. My dad has this old saying, "I pledge it." That means that you are not telling a lie. He is not fibbing to us. No matter what. It is not a joke. It's never teasing. And it's a really big deal if we don't tell the truth. And um, so, this boy called my sister. And I went into my parents' room. A friend and I had, at her house, learned how to unscrew the speaking thing on the telephone and take out the disk inside so that the person on the phone can't hear you talking but you can hear them. And I decided I was going to give it a shot. And I unscrewed it and I was listening to that phone conversation. And my dad came in. And uh, he just looked at me, and in my moment of fear, I told him that I was cleaning the telephone. Which was just ridiculous, but I told him that. And um, I've never seen him look so mad. And I've never been so scared of him. And then in thirty seconds, I told him the truth. And I said I was really eavesdropping. And I'm very sorry. And I got in so much trouble. And it was just such a blatant, blatant lie. And dad said that he wasn't mad at me for eavesdropping—that's just human nature. But that it was the lie that got me in trouble. I never felt so guilty about anything ever. And it had the worst repercussions. And it's something I'm still just embarrassed about. Something that we can't even joke about still, to this day.

--Lucinda

Lucinda's misdeed pales in comparison to Terry's. It was childish mischief--a Dennis the Menace kind of prank, with no potential for serious harm. Lucinda lied to a parent, just as Terry did, but Lucinda instantly recanted her lie and apologized in earnest. Lucinda, it seems, should let herself off the moral hook fairly easily. But instead she still dangles from it, almost a decade later.

In many families, stories such as Lucinda's become favorite tales, to be repeated with fondness and amusement to family and friends. Terry told us that her experience of driving the car into the living room became a prized family joke. Not so in Lucinda's family. Lucinda's father was rigid and humorless about matters of morality. I suspect that if it were Lucinda who had driven the car through the garage, she would still be paying for it, materially and emotionally. I think there is another consequence of unforgivingly high moral standards--they invite lies about misdeeds.

Lucinda lied about her misbehavior because she feared her father's fury. I think the main reason she confessed was not because her father's presence reminded her of her own deeply held moral convictions, but because her lie was so obviously implausible that she had no hope of getting away with it.

Chapter 8

Entitlement Lies:
Lying for What You Think You Deserve

This occurred about three years ago. At the time, I was a senior in high school and my boyfriend was 22. It happened around New Year's Eve. He got his sister to call up my mother and pretend that she was his mother and told my mother that I was staying out late with them and would be staying over at their house for New Year's Eve. And I got a friend of mine who pretended that she was my mother and called his mother and told her that Denny, my boyfriend, was staying over at my house for New Year's Eve. On New Year's Eve, we did go out with my boyfriend's parents. That much was true. Afterwards we went into the city and had more drinks but instead of going back to either house we wet to the Sheraton and we stayed there that night. And the thing that makes this so significant is that we were so scared of letting our parents get together that, I mean for almost a year I don't even think we let them talk to each other even over the phone. This just took so much planning and so it involved so many people. I have yet to understand how it came off as good as it did in a way. And um, I rarely lie to my parents and I only lied to them when I know that they would disapprove of something for the wrong reason or for a reason that is unacceptable to me. I think they would have said no because of moral reasons and my sense of morality is not the same as theirs. So I guess that's the way I justified it in my head—that they're trying to make me conform to a sense of morality that isn't my morality."

—Laura

Entitlement lies are told with moral aplomb. The tellers of these lies believe that they <u>should</u> be allowed to engage in a particular behavior or enjoy a certain privilege. If an authority from a different moral planet is likely to stand in the way, then they will simply dodge that alien with a lie.

Because the moral blockade is readily anticipated, entitlement lies tend to be planned in advance. The plans can be fairly simple ones, or, as in this instance, quite elaborate. These lies seem to have a fairly high rate of success. They probably succeed in part because they have been so carefully planned. But they also succeed because the liars are not consumed with guilt or shame, and therefore they are unlikely to show the anxiety or the apprehensive demeanor of the liar who feels morally vulnerable.

> Once you lie once, it's so easy...especially when you think it is for a good cause.

> Well, because I got away with it without that much damage maybe I thought I could lie again. Maybe it started me thinking that maybe lies weren't that bad.

> This was the first time I had really gotten away with anything. It made me realize that I can deceive my dad so like the rest of the summer I kept doing it. It kind of made me realize how easy it was and that it wasn't such a bad thing.

When the guilt-wracked eavesdropper of the earlier story discussed the aftermath of her lie, she said that she had learned "such a good lesson. I don't think I could ever lie to my dad again. It made me realize that I shouldn't even try it. It taught me that if I had just told the truth that the initial thing I was doing wasn't half as bad as the lie."

The tellers of entitlement lies learn lessons, too. But their lessons are that lying is easy, that it is a skill that can be practiced and learned and improved, and that it is really not such a bad thing. Although the three quotes directly above may sound very similar, they are from three different people. What the three people had in common was that they were all describing their reactions to telling an entitlement lie. There is a certain uniformity in the tone of the entitlement lies. Although there may have been some excitement and danger involved in pulling off the lie and sustaining it over time, there is a placidity about the act of lying. The attitudes of the tellers of the primitive lies are more variable. They range from the bemused air of the woman whose car ended up next to the living room couch, to the self-flagellating tone of the eavesdropper who could not stop telling us that she never felt so ashamed in her life.

Entitlement lies are especially characteristic of people for whom huge swatches of their lives are under the governance of authority figures. Therefore, it was not surprising that the college students in our research told many more of them than did the much older sample of people from the community. (Typically, the college students told their entitlement lies to their parents.) The people from the community, in turn, told relatively more instrumental lies.

Chapter 9

Instrumental Lies

There is no doubt many lies have passed through these lips over the years but the one I will attempt to relay is one I have never been able to dismiss from my mind. I was about one month into a job selling new and used cars. This day a man came in looking to buy a new car having a car to trade. Certainly a normal situation. However, after a few words with this man it was evident that he was more than a little inebriated. I had him look at some brochures while I checked with the sales manager who said, ' Sell him anyway,' and so I did. I showed several cars and he picked the one he wanted. We now got down to the financing; this is where the problem began. The man had two cars to trade on one new car. I felt sure this would be a bad deal for him especially in his condition, but I drew up the papers and again consulted the sales manager about the deal and his condition. The sales manager went into orbit. ' Sell him, sell him; we'll get one car free.' At that time the man's daughter walked in. She was the owner of one of the trade-in cars. She knew nothing about dealing on cars. It was at this point I could have taken her aside and told her how bad a deal her father was making and that in his condition he should go home, sober up, and come back. But I did not. Instead, I had both of them sign the papers and the sale was consummated. The following day the man and the daughter brought in the two cars and drove in the new car and I never heard a thing from them afterwards. They also lived close to where I lived at the time and I saw that car *often*. I figure this deal cost that hard working man thousands of dollars, and all to make a commission and please a sales manager."

-- Jimmy

Instrumental lies are the lies with pitchforks and horns. Liars tell them to get what they want, sometimes at someone else's expense. The people who participated in our research told us about lies they told to conceal shoplifted merchandise, to get to go to the prom with their most preferred date instead of the first person who asked, to get better grades than they deserved (the "prize" going to the woman who cheated on 15 consecutive quizzes), and to get more favorable returns on their taxes, loan applications, and court proceedings.

The tellers of instrumental lies are usually who people have in mind when they think of liars as cold and calculating. And some, in fact, are exactly that. For example, few tax cheats stay up nights agonizing over the fraud they have perpetrated on their nation's government. Yet not all instrumental lie-tellers are so cool. Some are like Jimmy, the car salesman quoted above, who lies and then squirms. His is an especially interesting story because he had so many supports for his lie. His sales manager sanctioned it not once but twice--and with excitement. Moreover, there is a script for selling cars that everyone knows--both the buyer and the seller are out to make the most profitable deal possible. No one expects salespersons to warn customers that they really could do better. Yet, years later, he still could not set his guilt aside.

In the research my colleagues and I conducted, we found few tellers of serious lies who expressed no misgivings whatsoever about their dishonesty. Liars who told lies of entitlement, and some who told instrumental lies, were mostly alone in their dispassionate perpetration of deceit.

Chapter 10

Lies About Passions

Early in July 1986, I went out to a local club to hear music and dance. While there I saw many acquaintances, including a couple I'll call Sue and Sam. Later, after midnight, Sue found me and said that Sam had left without her, so I offered to let her stay in my spare bedroom. She agreed. At my house, we reconsidered the arrangement, and decided we could sleep with each other, but fully clothed. Of course, this didn't work out, as it was the dead of summer, and we eventually made love, then put on a few light clothes. Around 8 a.m. Sam walked into my bedroom (I had neglected to lock my door) and confronted us. He was obviously upset, and shattered the glass in my front door. Sue was frantic, not knowing what effect this would have on Sam, and not wanting her 16-year old son to be exposed to any of it. I was faced with replacing my door to secure my home, escape from a horrible nightmare of a domestic incident, and arrive at my 6-year old daughter's first time on the stage at Children's Theater at 11. First I measured the door while Sue tried to call Sam. He answered but wouldn't talk. I put Sue in my truck, bought us each a beer, and went to the house they shared. Sam was withdrawn, not himself, in shock. I told him that Sue and I talked, that she told me things he needed to hear, that I was ashamed and without excuse for my behavior, and then I sincerely denied having had sex with his girlfriend. He politely asked me to leave. I drove to a local building supply, bought a new door, took it home, bathed, and made the play on time, in a somewhat exhilarated state. Later that day, Sam called me. He had talked to Sue, and believed my story, and did not want to give up his relationship with her, nor his friendship with me. As of now, six months later, this is still the case. I have often explained the sudden need to replace my front door by claiming that I slipped on the stairs, lost control of a folded card table which then cart-wheeled through the glass.

--Bob

Lies about affairs often occupy a different moral and emotional space than either primitive lies, entitlement lies, or instrumental lies. Their claim to specialness is the element of passion in the behaviors that the lies are hiding. In our culture, we like to think of emotions such as lust and love as forces that seize us, that wrestle us from our senses, and cause us to act uncontrollably against what we know to be our better judgment and our more characteristic integrity. Now all this may be a myth, but we live by it.

When people lie to cover the misdeeds prompted by their passions, they can try to tell themselves and even others that their bad behavior was not entirely premeditated. Bob and Sue let themselves nestle in the same bed, but only after they made the deliberate decision to remain fully clothed. What they did not anticipate was that their clothes would be torn from their bodies by the heat of the night and the throes of passion.

Bob and Sue's Excellent Adventure

One of the most striking aspects of this story about an affair is the liar's cavalier attitude. Here is someone who has just slept with one friend (Sue) who is a girlfriend of another friend (Sam), and as a consequence, has sent Sam away "in shock". Yet how does he describe his lie? Mostly, I'd say, as a thrilling adventure in which he emerges as the hero. Look at the challenges facing our daring adventurer. After sleeping with his friend's girlfriend (the only part of the story he describes as if it were boring), then getting caught in bed with her, he next has to make amends with Sam. In doing so, he gallantly tells him "things he needed to hear," things which Sue has entrusted to our hero during their few hours together, even though she has never told Sam, who is the person these things concern, and with whom she has had a much longer term intimate relationship. Sam initially sends Bob away, but then ponders the wisdom of what our hero liar has said and decides to call him with a tribute to his honor and his friendship: He announces that he believes Bob, and does not want to give up their friendship. (Note that what was described as an acquaintance before the affair becomes a cherished friendship after it.) Moreover, Sam continues to believe in Bob's innocence even after six months have passed.

Like most action heroes, Bob is totally in control. He is the person thinking up the great plots and executing the adventures. He saves a 16-year old from a devastating truth and a 6-year old from a deep disappointment. He is juggling a "horrible nightmare of a domestic incident" with the mundane details of repairing his front door, all under breath-taking time pressure. It seems that not even the simplest behaviors can be performed by other characters in this tale without the aid of hero Bob. How, for example, does the fully grown adult woman who has just slept with Bob end up in his truck? Bob "put" her there.

Even Bob's feelings are those of a hero rather than a philanderer. When at last he arrives at the play and sees his daughter, does he feel consumed with guilt and shame? No! He feels "exhilarated"! Does he feel twinges of humiliation every time he must explain the need to replace his front door? No! Instead, he seems to revel in the telling of his exciting lie, in which a card table "cartwheeled through the glass". What fun it is to lust and to lie! In reading and rereading the transcripts of the liars' accounts of their lies about affairs, it is hard to believe that they are describing the same kinds of events as the dupes were describing when they told about partners who cheated on them. When Rita said, "I felt as if my whole world had fallen away beneath me," she did not seem to be having very much fun.

If at First You Don't Succeed, Lie, Lie Again

When we asked the dupes what strategies they thought the liars had used to perpetrate their lies, the one they mentioned most often was that of telling even more lies. Examination of the liars' own stories leads to much the same conclusion. By his own admission, Bob lied repeatedly to Sam at the time of the confrontation and then never did anything to undo the lie in the months that followed. He also amused himself with the lie that he told to any number of other people about the need to replace his front door. Many liars are just like Bob in the way that they tell lie upon lie. They lie to bolster the first lie, to set the stage for subsequent lies, and to fend off accusations and recriminations. Further, as the tale of the elaborate New Year's Eve ploy indicated, sometimes liars even recruit other people to lie on their behalf.

Chapter 11

Identity Lies:
Becoming a Different Person

I come from a small Southern town and this university's a lot bigger than my high school was. In high school I was one of the big shots, very important in government and things like that. When I came here I kind of felt like a little fish in a big pond and so I embellished on my high school life to an incredible extent. I said I played state championship football in high school and I even threw in a bit of sympathy ploy by implying that I'd been hurt very badly before my senior year and that's why I couldn't play any more. I also said that I'd played baseball and was offered some baseball scholarships to various schools but I came to UVA because it was a very fine academic institution and all. The main problem being when I came to school I was very set in my ways; had a girlfriend back home; kinda thought I was going to go back home after I finished here and get a job in my hometown. Everything would be all fine and dandy. What's happened now is I have a very serious girlfriend here who goes home on occasion with me. And, um, when I go home, it's interesting because I feel like I have to try to keep things from her. A lot of my friends who I'm still very close with, I'm always worried that she's going to say something to them like, it must have been great knowing him when he was the star on the football team. Um, another problem being that my friends more than expected have come up here to visit me, go see games, or you know, just come visit for a weekend. And, um, it seems to create a lot of tension because I'm always worried that they're going to say something to my roommates who are also party to this lie because they think I was Joe Hotshot back in high school. Basically, that's my story. I've deceived a lot of people and a lot of times I'm very very apprehensive and I worry that either my girlfriend who I'm very serious with is going to find out, or some of my friends are going to find out, and I'm going to be made a fool out of."

--Paul

Going away to college, for many adolescents, is a deeply significant life event. They leave behind their friends and family, the comfortable familiarity of people and places, and venture into a new domain. For some, the experience is exciting and liberating. They are free not only from the rules and sanctions of their earlier life, but also from the expectations of all those people who know them well. In the company of strangers, they can mold their identity anew. The class clown can become the studious intellectual; the serious, responsible student can become the carefree nonconformist. These kinds of changes are forward looking. Those who attempt them do not rewrite their high school life histories; rather, they pen a new script for college.

For other adolescents such as Paul, the young man in the present story who is moving from the small pond of a little school in a little town to the vast ocean of big-time university life, the prospect of establishing himself in a sea of strangers is more intimidating than liberating. As he said when we asked him why he told his lie, "I lied because I felt insecure and I felt like I needed an edge to get people to like me, you know, coming to this new school." Many identity lies are borne of just such fear and insecurity. The tellers of identity lies usually do <u>not</u> fit the stereotype of liars as bold, brazen, cold, and manipulative people who are out to exploit others in order to satisfy their selfish desires. Instead, they are people such as Paul, who want so badly just to fit in, to be liked, to be respected as much as the next guy, but who fear that their unadorned self is just too wanting to achieve even these modest goals. They are intimidated and they are scared. And so they lie, not simply by telling a single, clear-cut, one-time lie, but by creating a whole new self that thrives on lies.

The result is that you present an image of yourself not as what you are, but what you would like to be in your wildest fantasy.

Identity lies, more than any other kinds, are wishful, fanciful lies. The liars want themselves to be certain kinds of people so badly that they simply make that happen by force of deceit. By lying, they make their wishes come true.

Paul's lie eventually transformed itself from a dream come true into a nightmare. However, in its initial form, in the context in which it first took shape, it was not such a badly crafted deceit. Paul was in a new place with all new people. What he lied about was his past--something that happened in a different place at a different time in front of a different audience. He even built in certain protections against being called on to live up to his lies. For example, he created for himself the serious injury that kept him on the sidelines during his senior year. He describes this as a sympathy ploy, but it was also of strategic significance. It cautioned his new friends not to expect any dazzling athletic performances in his current life.

Paul also expected to be protected by his life plans. He would get his college education, then return to his home town where he would find a job, marry his high school sweetheart, and live happily ever after. When university life proved more broadening than this, the lie that once seemed so well insulated was suddenly open to attack. Now his girlfriend was a college student who could come home with him and meet his friends who knew what he was really like in high school. And his high school friends could come to visit him at college and learn what his new friends think he was like in high school. Instead of living comfortably in his new lie, he had to be on guard constantly to protect and defend it.

At least in the movies, identity dreams can come true. If Paul had complete control of his life script, he probably would have written something similar to the movie "Dave", in which a man-on-the-street is plucked out of his humdrum, anonymous existence to fill in for a physically impaired president. Initially, Dave was chosen merely for his uncanny physical resemblance to the president, and he felt stiff and insecure in the role. But gradually, he grew into it, and became a far more effective and beloved leader than the "real" president he had replaced.

> Sometimes I feel as though she's in love with something that isn't the truth, and if she ever did find out, maybe she won't like me for what I am.

Real life is rarely as kind as the movies. Paul never did grow into the person that he had hewn for himself. Perhaps even more tragically, he never experienced the deep gratification of coming into a new and challenging situation and earning acceptance for who he really was. Of course, his fear was that his true self would not have merited that acceptance. But this fear may have been misplaced.

Paul never did learn whether his friends, including even his new girlfriend, may have actually liked his true self better than his fanciful one. During our interview with him, it appeared that such a possibility never even occurred to him. Other tellers of identity lies, in contrast, actually did discover that the self they manufactured was, ironically, <u>less</u> appealing to its audience than their "true" self would have been. For example, the young man quoted above who "didn't want to seem like a little dork" made up a new self to present to his very first girlfriend. He created old girlfriends so that his first love would think he was an experienced man of the world. Although he didn't drink at all, he concocted a past filled with drunken adventures, so that the love of his life would be filled with awe. But when she began to talk about her life, she said that unlike him, she had hardly any experience at romance and was not much of a drinker. It didn't take him long to come to the wistful realization that she may well have found that "little dork" far more endearing than the swaggering lustful drunk he only pretended to have been.

The Work of Lying

| I think I was silly for feeling that insecure when I came here but I feel trapped by it right now.

When people, out of fear or longing, create the new selves that they "would like to be in [their] wildest fantasies," they sometimes find that what they have fashioned is not the stylish and enviable self of their dreams, but an insatiable monster. Fabricated selves have voracious appetites; they can only thrive if they are fed more and more and more lies. And the more they stuff themselves with deceit, the more bloated they become. These false and boastful selves begin to take up much of the psychic space that rightfully belongs to the former selves that were never this greedy.

Sustaining the new self, which demands the relentless telling of lies, becomes hard work. In our interview with Paul, he went on to describe the tortured existence he led when he was alone with his new friends, when his old friends came to the university, and when his university friends went home with him. "If conversations start swaying back to high school, I try to interrupt them and sway them to something else--popular music or something like that. When my old friends are here I try to keep them isolated from my new friends as much as possible. I try to go out with them and do things with them and try not to include my college roommates, my friends, or my girlfriends with things I do with them...when my college friends come home with me, I feel like I have to try to be a sneak and not let them find out what I was really like." There was no rest, no peace of mind, no easy integration of past and present lives for this liar.

From the outside, it may appear that the obvious solution to this agony is simply to come clean. But the cruel irony of these fabricated selves is that they are far more readily created than dismantled. In this way, the psychological task of fashioning a new identity is disarmingly similar to the physical experience of regulating weight. It is easy to gain weight but hard to lose it. Although new selves are initially under the control of their creators, they ultimately develop lives of their own. Other people learn about the new and untrue selves, they tell still others about these untrue people, who perhaps tell even more people. Thus, the tellers of identity lies who contemplate the possibility of reclaiming their true selves do indeed feel trapped. For these liars to undo just those lies they are directly responsible for perpetrating would itself be a formidable task. But even if that could be achieved, it would not be enough. For the lies they hatched sired their own little lies, and those new generations of lies scurried off to places unknown and untraceable.

Designing Swatches of the Self:
Mini-Identity Lies

Perhaps my reader won't be of the opinion that the following was a very important lie. Perhaps it wasn't. But to me it was very serious indeed. When one reflects that I told it more than fifty years ago and still have a vivid and unhappy memory of it, perhaps it will qualify as being important. It was to me. I was living in the North then and dating a most attractive man from Louisiana. In fact, I rather thought that I might want to marry him one day. I confided that I wrote quite a lot (which was true) and had had some of my things accepted and published in a prestigious magazine. In point of fact, I had never even submitted anything to them.

--Bonnie

Many lies about identity are not full blown recreations of the self but instead are redesigns of mere swatches of the self--often just a single fact. The above story, told by a 71-year old woman, is an example of such a mini-identity lie. Her experience is remarkable because by most objective criteria the lie she told was not very serious, yet she reports that she continues to feel troubled by it a half-century later. Her experience is reminiscent of Lucinda's. The misdeed that Lucinda committed was merely to listen in on her older sister's telephone conversation, then tell a quick lie that was immediately recanted; yet the agony that followed this experience was relentless. The longstanding emotional reactions that these liars endured are important to keep in mind when we are tempted to dismiss all liars as cold and heartless.

Bonnie's lie about her publishing achievements was similar to Paul's in that it grew out of a desperate desire to be a more accomplished and impressive person than she thought she really was. And her interpersonal goals, like Paul's, seemed to be acceptance, inclusion, and love. In her case, her lie was directed at the person who at that point may have been the most important person in her life--the man she thought she might marry.

Other mini-identity lies, however, have a somewhat different flavor. They serve not to create a new and more impressive self, but to hide some personal attribute, fact, or condition that the liar feels would be distressing for the dupe to know. One liar, for example, never told anyone in his family that he was seriously injured during the war. Another liar withheld from her elderly mother the fact that she had Parkinson's disease. Motivationally, these liars are not out to enhance their self-images but to protect some other person. Typically, the person being protected is someone near and dear to them, who would probably feel some rightful claim to knowing these hidden truths, and who may not feel so grateful for the protection.

Chapter 12

Taking a Fall:
Lies Told to Cover for Someone Else

About a year ago my best friend got involved really heavily with this guy and they started fooling around and everything and she got pregnant. And she was only 17, so of course, we were going to get an abortion for her. And she's pretty scatterbrained so I pretty much set the whole thing up and I made the appointment and I took her there and everything, you know, was fine. On that Saturday, we told her mom that she was just gonna spend the night at my house after we cheered because a lot of times after a game, she'd spend the night there. We were just going to go early in the morning and get it done and we did and everything was fine and she had to go back for more check-up's and they gave her some kind of medicine in case any infection or anything came in. She kept the receipt for it in her purse, and her parents found it and they knew that someone had had an abortion. So they asked us about it together one night at dinner and we said it was me. And her parents decided not to tell my parents. And this was about a year ago and it comes up all the time and so I had to tell a whole bunch of lies about that. And I had to say it was me, to their face, and that she was the one that took me and we just pretty much reversed all the roles. Maria was my best friend and her parents are very very Catholic—she even had an uncle who was a priest—and there's just no way they could have ever accepted that she did that."

—Katie

Some of the most astounding stories we collected were ones such as Katie's in which one person takes the rap for what some would consider to be a gravely serious deed. Maria had an abortion. Katie's lie was to tell Maria's parents that it was she, and not Maria, who had the abortion.

The costs to Katie of telling this lie were enduring and profound. Before the lie, Maria's parents "loved her hanging around with me. I had always been the one they brought up to Maria to show what a good example I was." Katie and Maria were next-door neighbors and Katie loved going over to Maria's house. But afterwards, "I didn't like going over there as much...sometimes I felt like I shouldn't be there...that they just looked down on me."

Katie told her own parents about the lie, and then she had problems with their reaction, too. Unsurprisingly, they thought that Maria, and not Katie, should have taken responsibility for Maria's actions: "They'd bring it up a lot, and tell me that I shouldn't have done that, and I'd get really defensive about it."

Katie was also left to wrestle with her own moral and emotional reactions to the lie: "A lot of times, I tried to talk to myself and make myself believe one hundred percent that what I did was right, and that there was no possibility that I did the wrong thing." Katie told us again and again throughout the interview that if she had it to do over, she would tell the lie again. Yet the issue seems far from settled in her heart or in her mind.

> You're such a high pillar of principle that even your deputies can't tell you the truth...you punish people with your righteousness.
> --Dr. Brock to her husband the sheriff, in *Picket Fences*

Maria's family, I think, was morally and ethically complex and not without hypocrisy. The most blatant moral dimension was their obvious religiosity. Theirs was, as Katie told us repeatedly, a very very religious family--a family which even included a clergyman. "Thou shalt not have an abortion", "Thou shalt not engage in such behaviors that might raise the issue of abortion", and "Though shalt not lie" were the commandments of that family, as well as of the church. This was a family that insisted on righteousness and truth, and I suspect that, ironically, it was just such insistence that made it so difficult for their daughter to tell the truth.

There are hints in this tale, though, that Maria's parents do not live up to their own high standards. Why, for example, were they snooping in Maria's purse?   And why do they confront Maria with their discovery of the receipt at the dinner table in the presence of Maria's best friend? Maria lived in a very confusing and difficult family environment.

Cheerleading at Night, Abortion in the Morning

In pondering this tale, my colleagues and I were moved by the starkly contrasting images from these young women's lives. At night, they were bouncy peppy cheerleaders adored by the roaring crowds. They were teenagers enjoying the utter frivolity of high school life. In the morning, they were all by themselves, grimly facing an invasive and potentially terrifying medical procedure, an emotionally explosive moral issue, and the beginnings of a deep dark secret that they would try to hide from their parents and all of their friends.

How did Katie deal with this? Her strategy was oddly reminiscent of Bob's. She took charge. She was the detail person. She managed the logistics of this serious life event which she just assumed her "scatterbrained" friend would be incapable of handling for herself.   Perhaps this immersion in the minutia of the planning of the act helped her to avoid a more painful confrontation with the deeper and broader meanings and implications of the life event that was unfolding.

How to Succeed at Lying Without Really Trying

Whether by brilliance or luck, Katie and Maria came up with a stunningly effective strategy for telling a successful lie. In relating every single detail--except the most crucial one--they simply told the truth. The only untrue fact in their story was the identity of the person who had the abortion. It was Maria, but they claimed it was Katie. All of the other facts of the matter could be reeled off effortlessly and truthfully. Although Katie and Maria did decide ahead of time that if they were ever challenged that Katie would take the blame, they needed no further planning to ensure the success of their lie. No one needed to memorize a cover story, because the story they told was a true one. They were both participants in this real life event, and so they could both describe how the event in fact unfolded. They did not need to coordinate their stories. And subsequently, they did not need to make any special effort to remember what it was that they had or had not said to Maria's parents, because they simply told the truth. In the tale of Maria and Katie, the truth was the best lie.

Chapter 13

Living a Lie

This is a lie I lived for 20 years. My husband and I separated in 1958. I was working for the government in Washington, D.C. He left me there and came to Waynesboro to live. I stayed on there until 1978 when I retired after 30 years service. At first I did not want the people where I worked to know that my husband had left me, so I never told anyone. Any time they asked me to go anywhere I used the excuse that I had to go home to fix dinner for my husband. When we had luncheons or farewell parties for any of the workers, I told them my husband never liked to go to anything like that.

I was working with the Navy, so like any men, after you work with them for a while they try to see if you will go out with them. I always told them I had a very jealous husband and got rid of them that way. I did not want to be bothered with another man so I decided to never tell them I was single. There were a lot of times I had to tell them he was out of town. I never discussed my home life at work. Everyone assumed I was happily married and I let them think just that. Even at my retirement party I told them he was working out of town and was not able to come. My family all knew we were separated but they were all down here. They never saw anyone up there where I worked. When I retired I moved to Staunton, right near Waynesboro, to take care of my mother who passed away last June. I have never in all this time seen my ex-husband anywhere here in town. I know he is here."

—Helen

This phenomenal lie is one of the best examples described to us of the category of "living a lie". It is an identity lie of a very special kind--one that pertained to the core of the liar's identity, that she told to untold numbers of dupes, and that she perpetrated for 20 years. It is also remarkable that Helen described her breathtakingly bold lie in a rather matter-of-fact tone. Some of the lies described by the dupes also would qualify as examples of "living a lie"; in fact, there were more lies of this nature in their tales than in the liars'. But the dupes were not nearly so dispassionate about them. Once again, liars and targets of lies, even when discussing very similar kinds of lies, seem to be describing very different experiences.

PART 4

Lessons for Liars and Dupes

Chapter 14

Tips for turning down the heat on deceit

As I read and reread the transcripts of all of these stories of serious lies, it became evident that the tellers of serious lies are in some ways self-enabling. There are certain things they tell themselves that ease them down liars lane. I've collected those self-deceptions here. Maybe readers who peruse them will, in the future, be less likely to give in to their own temptations to tell big-time lies. In the pages ahead, I will also share some suggestions for liars who want to come clean, spell out some tips for truth-tellers, and explain why some of the most unlikely people can end up as dupes.

Lies That Liars Tell Themselves

Thinking of lying? Join the club. Many people who find themselves in a difficult or threatening situation are tempted to try to lie their way out of their troubles. To liars, lies are like wishes. If only their lies really were true, life would be so much kinder, more indulgent, and carefree. And so liars egg themselves on, by telling themselves the following lie myths. I think they are best considered as self-deceptions--lies that liars tell themselves.

#1. **"I can get away with this lie."**

Few liars embark upon the telling of a serious lie thinking that they are going to get caught. More commonly, they think they can pull it off. My advice to them is, "Don't count on it." Despite their generally high expectations for getting away with their lies, about 40% of the liars in our research were eventually found out.

Liars can develop an inflated view of their chances of success not only because they overestimate their own lie-telling skills, but also because they fail to appreciate the extent to which the fate of their lies is out of their control. If just one other person is in on the lie, if just one other person knows about the lie, or if just one other person knows about the bad behavior that the lie was meant to hide, then all of the lie-telling skills in the world will not save the liar from the risk that the lie will be leaked by that one other person.

Liars usually do realize that the targets of their lies can become suspicious and then try to check out their suspicions. But they are not always fully tuned in to the magnitude of those suspicions or the extensiveness of the target's efforts to learn the truth. Further, some dupes are adept at hiding their suspicions; thus, they can be getting closer and closer to the truth as the liar remains blissfully oblivious. This combination of a clueless liar and a shrewd and sensitive dupe often ends on a shocking note for the liars--they discover all at once that they have been completely undone.

> Even when you think you'll not get caught, there's a good chance you will and it's better just to be honest.

> Just don't lie.

Telling a successful serious lie is a lot like trying to commit the perfect crime. Many try it, but far fewer succeed. Even with meticulous planning, not every twist and turn can be anticipated. Lindy, the woman who reneged on a dinner engagement with her boyfriend to go out to dinner with another guy, went to a restaurant that her boyfriend never frequented. Of course, her boyfriend decided to go to just that restaurant that evening. Fine--Lindy would simply dive under the table. She did, but she could not remain perfectly still, and so her lie was undone by the quivering tablecloth. And what of the religion professor? What odds would he have given that his wife Rita would find the necklace in his briefcase, that his secretary would wear it to the theater the next evening, and that he and his wife would run into her during intermission? In any lie, as in any crime, the number of cues that need to be controlled and tracks that need to be covered turns out to be infinite.

#2. "No one will ever challenge me – I'll make sure of it."

The second myth that liars live by is lying by intimidation. Liars who have a reputation for being angry, mean, and vindictive may in fact be overtly challenged less often than are kinder and gentler liars. The fallacy in this strategy, though, is that an absence of challenge is not the same as an absence of suspicion or even of detection. The dupe who has discovered the deceit of an irascible liar may well be too scared to confront the liar with the facts. As a consequence, it is the liar who is left unknowingly playing without a full deck. The target of the lie knows the score, but the liar does not know that the target knows.

One of the most agonizing stories told by the dupes was Patty's. Patty and her sister were caught in the midst of a bitter battle between their estranged parents over which parent the children would stay with that weekend. Patty ended up pushed into the car of her father and stepmother and whisked away, leaving her and her sister separated for the first time in their lives. Patty was crying uncontrollably. After a while, her stepmother got her to stop crying by stopping the car and enlisting the help of a police officer, who came to the car and told Patty that if she did not stop crying, he was going to put her in jail. This is an example of lying by intimidation. The stepmother was infamous for her temper, and so

Patty kept her suspicions to herself for years. Until Patty finally confronted her stepmother more than a decade later, the liar never knew for sure that Patty still remembered the incident, figured out the lie, and remained forever resentful.

It is not only anger and ill-temper that can silence the open expression of a dupe's suspicions. The treat of any noxious emotional expression can similarly scare off challenges and confrontations. Some liars make it achingly clear to the targets that if they were ever suspected of deceit, their feelings would be mortally wounded. The dupes who hear that message may well decide to keep their suspicions to themselves so as not to have to deal with a wounded and moping whiner; but again, that does not stop them from having their suspicions nor from definitively uncovering the deceit. It simply leaves the liars in the dark as to whether and when they been undone.

#3. **"Even if my lie is discovered, I can make it up to the person I deceived. Eventually, we can have just as good a relationships as we had before."**

Over and done. Ancient history. That's what liars like to tell themselves about the lies they told that were found out. But when we as researchers heard the emotions in the voices and in the words of the people who had been deceived as they told their tales, it did not seem to us that the episodes were "over and done" for them.

When lies are used to cover massive betrayals of intimacy, such as longstanding affairs, the consequences for the relationship of the discovery of the lies can be profound or even fatal. Trust is tarnished, resentment seeps in, and sometimes the relationship is forever severed by the weight of the misery.

For short term things like having Sam for the weekend, lying was good, but the long term effects were bad: My parents lost trust in me.

In the long run, I think it has hurt both of us even more than if I had just told the truth in the beginning.

The consequences of any betrayal need to be considered in the context of the relationship. The hurt that we heard in the dupes' voices and in their stories seemed especially intense when the person who lied to them was the first person they ever dated, or the first person with whom they ever slept, or the first person to whom they ever expressed their deepest emotions. Any person with an extraordinarily special place in another person's life takes on an especially great risk that their misbehaviors will be less readily forgiven, and their lies less readily forgotten, by the person who has been betrayed by them.

My colleagues and I were also struck by the indelible marks left by lies told to cover even fairly minor transgressions. One mother, for example, told us about a time when her daughter was caught trying to sneak to a forbidden dance under the cover of babysitting for the couple up the street. Her lie was undone when her father decided to walk her to the couple's home. The lie, her mother said, "has made it more difficult for us to take her word for something and we tend to have traces of distrust in circumstances where we would ordinarily have given her the benefit of the doubt." Lies told to cover small misbehaviors such as this one become especially meaningful and lasting in their implications when they mark turning points in relationships. The good and dutiful daughter turns out to be a liar and a sneak. Now when she says she is going babysitting or to the meeting of the journalism club or to a friend's house after school, eyebrows are raised and doubts fester. Eventually, the daughter can become resentful, too, if she feels that she is being tortured mercilessly about a minor misstep.

Sometimes relationships do survive serious lies. In some instances, they are even strengthened by the process of struggling through and beyond them. And sometimes people win million dollar lotteries. But both are long shots. The only way to ensure that your relationship will not be damaged by a serious lie is to not tell it.

#4. "I have their best interests in mind. "

Liars love to claim that they have the dupes' best interests at heart. There are different versions of this claim. Liars might insist that the persons they are deceiving really do not want to know the truth, or cannot handle the truth, or would welcome the lie.

Some uses of this plea seem especially gratuitous. Thelma, one of our dupes, told us about a time in her life when she was infatuated with a guy she knew. Thelma confided to her friend Susan that she longed to become involved with this guy. Soon afterwards, Susan told Thelma that her dream was about to come true--her Prince was going to ask her to the prom. A few days later, when Thelma saw Prince Charming, he excitedly announced to her: "Guess who I am taking to the prom--Gertrude!" When Thelma subsequently confronted Susan with her anger and hurt, Susan replied that she told Thelma this lie because she knew that Thelma so desperately wanted to hear it.

Unsurprisingly, Thelma did not agree that her best interests were being served by Susan's lie. If she had been given a choice, she would have spared herself from Susan's "good intentions". Rare indeed would be the person who would choose those few days of misguided delight at the cost of the ultimate disappointment.

Other lies described by liars as protective, though, are less easily dismissed. Of all of the categories of lies we have considered--including all of the types of lies described by the dupes and all of the types described by the liars--none were so tightly wrapped in the cloak of presumed protectiveness as the lies about death and serious illnesses. Almost all of the targets who were misled, misinformed, or uninformed about the death or serious illness of a loved one believed that the liars were trying to protect them. Yet none of them appreciated this "protection." They felt that it robbed them of important opportunities to say their farewells, and it also robbed them of the dignity of being treated as an emotionally competent person.

It would be rash to conclude that because all of our dupes resented the death and illness lies that they were told, no one should ever mislead anyone else about such matters. Some people do in fact want such devastating news postponed as long as possible. For example, when I asked my mother whether she resented the fact that her family never told her that her mother was dying, she said that she did not; rather, she appreciated the prolonging of her glimmer of hope.

Liars who believe that their lies are in the best interests of the people they are deceiving should ask themselves why they believe this. Did the dupe ever tell them specifically that they would prefer to be spared certain truths? If not, liars should consider seriously how their lie will in fact be received. Will the targets feel "protected" or resentful? What opportunities will they miss out on if they are kept in the dark? Are the liars protecting the targets from pain or just postponing that pain? If the latter, would the targets appreciate the delay? And are the liars really protecting the dupes from a painful experience, or are they protecting themselves from having to deal with the depths of the dupes' emotional reactions?

#5. "I'm going to tell – later."

> It was hard getting the courage to tell her. I had to say, ' I've been dishonest to you for two or three years.' That's hard.

Like another well known road, the road to deceit is also paved with good intentions. Liars probably know that they are better off owning up to their lie than letting it be discovered by the target. For that reason and perhaps others as well, many liars tell themselves that they do plan to come clean about their lie--but not just yet. Liars like to tell themselves that they just need to get a little distance, or they just need a little time, or they need to wait until the circumstances of the dupe's life are just right for learning about the lie, or the circumstances of their life are just right for the confessing of the lie, or or or or or...

But as time passes and the lie remains undetected and unsuspected, it becomes more and more tempting simply to leave well enough alone. But this, too, is risky business. The liar's perception that all is well may be completely erroneous. It is possible that the target's suspicions have been building and incriminating evidence has been cumulating. If the liar waits too long, the lie will be let out of the bag by the dupe (or by someone who tattles to the dupe) instead of by the liar. By that time, the liar's protest, "but I was planning to tell you," will seem lame.

#6. "This is just between the two of us."

Liars like to think that there are only two parties to the lie--the liar and the dupe. They might concede that a limited degree of damage could occur within their relationship with the person they are deceiving, but they think that such damage, and any repercussions whatsoever of the lie, are contained within that one relationship.

This, too, is wishful thinking. Ask Jeannie's little sister. Jeannie is the liar whose parents imposed no formal curfew during her high school years but did ask her to come home a little early one night because of the treacherous weather conditions. Instead she came in at four in the morning and upon finding her mother still awake and worried about her, attempted one implausible lie after another. The consequence was not only that Jeannie had curfews imposed from that time on, but so did her younger sister. In fact, her sister never was given the freedom that Jeannie had enjoyed for years.

It is also wishful thinking for liars to believe that the damage to their reputations is limited to the darkened opinion harbored by the dupes. Liars risk being viewed skeptically by anyone the liars tried to enlist to perpetrate the lie, and by anyone who learned about the lie. Perhaps liars also disinhibit others from lying to them. One of the liars in our research summarized her lie in two sentences: "I was having an affair with a married man. When it appeared that this relationship was not going to result in a long term relationship, I began dating another person and did not tell my 'lover'." This person's lie was to cheat on the liar who was cheating on his wife.

Moral philosophers such as Sissela Bok believe that the telling of lies causes large scale damage to the moral fabric of society. They believe that it erodes the foundations of truthfulness and trust that are essential to civilization. I think their point may be overstated when used to characterize the domain of everyday lies, but it may have some merit with regard to the realm of serious lies.

#7. "If I can get away with this lie, there will be no costs to telling it."

Most people who are about to tell a serious lie have no idea just how much *work* it is to maintain the lie. They are obsessively preoccupied with escaping detection, and insistently tell themselves that if only they can forever avoid detection, all will be well. I do not think this is merely self-deception. Rather, would-be liars are often genuinely oblivious to the intensity and the scope of the burdens of concealment. They don't realize how hard it is to protect their serious lie until they've tried.

> Eventually I ended up quitting lying just because of fear of being discovered.

> The anxiety I experienced—I don't ever want to go through that again.

> I would hesitate to lie like that again, just because it took so much planning, and I had so much anxiety, that I didn't even think it was worth it.

As long as their lies remains hidden, liars live under the constant threat that someday someone will stumble upon them or dig them up. If the liars live, work, or socialize with people who are most likely to discover the lies, then the liars are stuck doing constant maintenance work to keep their lies well protected and in good repair. They may need to tell lots more lies to cover the first big one, and then, once they do that, they need to do all the work of trying always to remember which particular lies they told to which particular people (and which of those people may have repeated their lies to which other people). This is hard work, it is annoying, and it takes up mental space that most people would far prefer to devote to more comforting thoughts. What's more, it can be a source of great anxiety and stress. Many people who are nurturing a serious lie are living their lives in fear.

> It just made me feel so bad about lying that I try not to do it.

> I still haven't found a way to close it up in my mind, to close it up in my heart...maybe one day it will all just go away.

> After that, I just couldn't stand to have a lie like that on my conscience.

Even if their lies are never discovered, many liars still need to deal with their own guilt and shame. The process of perpetuating the lie can also perpetuate the guilt and the shame. Like fear, guilt and shame are burdensome not only because they are distressing and unpleasant feelings in and of themselves, but also because they crowd out of the liars' minds and hearts other thoughts and feelings that would be far more welcome. The collected burdens of maintaining lies--the anxiety, fear, guilt, and shame that liars experience, together with all the thinking they have to do to remember their lies and keep them straight--have a largely unanticipated consequence. They make liars insensitive and stupid. So much of their attention, effort, emotion, and thought is wrapped up in the perpetuation of their lie, that not enough is left over for the more gratifying and constructive uses of thinking and feeling in everyday life.

> I felt relieved that I had started telling her the truth.

> I felt better about myself that I was finally being honest, that I was a better person.

> After confessing, my thoughts were clear.

Sometimes liars are not fully aware of just how badly they had been feeling about their lies, and just how much work it had been to maintain their lies, until they finally do confess. Then they notice, sometimes with a bit of amazement, just how relieved they suddenly feel. Their thoughts are cleared, their consciences are cleansed, and their relationships are renewed.

> His praise only drove Lila away from him, and it made her realize that if you haven't told someone the truth for a long enough time, after a while you can't tell him anything at all and expect him to understand.
>
> --*Fortune's Daughter*, Alice Hoffman

In the novel *Fortune's Daughter*, Lila has concealed from her husband during the entire length of their courtship and marriage a deeply significant event in her life: that she once had a child, and gave her up for adoption. Lila's husband just can't understand why Lila is reluctant to be a labor coach for her pregnant friend. Wistfully, Lila realizes that although all she meant to do was to hide a piece of her past, what she in fact did was to make it impossible for her husband ever to truly understand her.

Serious lies that go undiscovered are like poltergeist in haunted houses. The parties to the lies, like the inhabitants of the houses, feel that there is some strange invisible force unnerving them and keeping them from ever feeling totally comfortable with each other. The force is called deceit.

The costs of concealment are not the liar's alone. People who were enlisted in the telling of the lie, and confidants who were told about the lie, are usually pledged to secrecy. They, too, suffer the burdens of not telling. If these confidants and co-conspirators have their own ties to the dupes, then they have been asked not just to help the liar, but also to betray the dupe. This, too, can cause resentment, and it is the liars who (rightfully) will bear the brunt of it.

#8. **"I can't deal with this."**

Consider these dilemmas:

- After you and your high school girlfriend have imbibed far too much alcohol, you take over the driving (though you do not yet have your license) and steer the car into a ditch. The car is totaled and both of you are covered with blood. Time to call the parents.

- Your friend desperately wants to buy a new house, but he doesn't have the money for the down payment. He asks to borrow it from you. You don't want to lend it to him and know you probably won't. But it is so difficult to say so.

- You have just arrived at the university, feeling insecure about coming from a small school in a small town, and you are craving acceptance and even a bit of recognition by your new peer group. You don't think your own modest accomplishments will be sufficient to win their esteem and affection.

- Your girlfriend was away so you decided to turn to another friend "for companionship and comfort". Her company was indeed comforting. Now your girlfriend is back, and is asking you about your weekend.

- "Your grandmother is dying." This is what you need to tell your daughter, who has had such a warm, loving, and special relationship with your own mother. This is what you have not yet told her.

The predicaments just described are examples of ones that faced the liars in our research. They are frightening, saddening, distressing, even harrowing situations. It is easy to imagine the liars in all of these scenarios (and many more) saying to themselves, "I can't deal with this." Who would not feel at least a twinge of temptation <u>not</u> to deal with these situations truthfully, but to try lie your way out of them? A serious lie is born when people are caught in these scary situations that rivet their attention on the painful present and make them feel that they would do anything to escape it--even lie. Especially lie. The here-and-now orientation of anxious, insecure, and frightened mortals is treacherous to the truth.

The perilous present, though, is just the beginning for those who choose the path of deceit. For even if they survive the moment by their lies, they will then be forced to face the relentless burdens of concealment throughout the foreseeable future.

It is not only the costs of concealment that can escalate as the lie continues for weeks and months and maybe even years. So can the consequences of discovery. Dupes who have been suckered over the long term may be far more angry, vengeful, hurt, and unforgiving, when at last they finally discover the lie, than they would have been if the liar had fessed up immediately (or better still, had never told the lie in the first place). These intense reactions to long-lived lies are especially likely to occur when the misdeeds covered by the lies were of personal importance to the targets (for example, most dupes are more personally offended by affairs than by smashed cars) and when they were repeated offenses, rather than one-time misdemeanors.

To avoid the burden of maintaining a lie, and the risk of upheaval if the lie is discovered, would-be liars must stand up and face the menacing music. Only then can they get it to stop.

Lie No Longer:
How to Come Clean

Perhaps the cautionary notes about the eight lies that liars tell themselves have come too late for you--you have already told your lie. But now you feel sufficiently concerned that you would like to come clean. How should you do it? Here are some suggestions.

#1. **Get clean and be willing to stay clean.** If the misbehavior that is being covered by your lie is still in progress, put an end to it. A permanent end. Don't bother to gear up for a pious confession of infidelity if you plan to adjourn immediately for your next romp in the hay.

#2. **Admit to the person you duped that your behavior was bad.** You can try to explain how you got yourself into such a rotten mess, but if you do not admit that it really was a mess, you will still seem a little bit stinky.

#3. **Show remorse.** Your remorse, guilt, and pain over having inflicted such a wound on the dupe is partial compensation for your misbehavior and your lie. Your distress redistributes the emotional burdens of your misbehaviors. Now you are both suffering. Moreover, your remorse is further evidence that you really do believe that your transgressions and your lies were despicable. Dupes want to know that.

#4. **Promise never to do it again. (And mean it-- see #1.)** Remember that you did something bad and you also lied about it. You are not in a very enviable position. It will not be enough to say you are sorry. You have to promise never to do it again.

#5. **Don't expect applause.** If you find it in your heart to own up to your tainted deeds and the lies that you told to hide them, to repudiate those misdeeds, to apologize for them, and to vow never to behave so badly ever again, perhaps you deserve a gracious, loving, forgiving response. Don't count on it. If you plan to come clean, you should be prepared to thrive solely on the self-satisfaction of your own reclaimed honesty and integrity. If, in addition, you are rewarded with a kind and generous response by the dupe, that's extra.

Tips for Truth-Tellers:
How to Help Yourself Avoid the Temptation to Tell Serious Lies

> I cannot face this thing inside of myself.

> The reason we are not used to telling the truth is that we are not used to facing it.
> --David Nyberg, *The Varnished Truth*

There is no more sobering section of this book than this one. All of the suggestions I will offer for avoiding the temptation to tell a serious lie, and for steeling yourself to tell the truth instead, are difficult ones to follow. I wish there were a magic bullet I could offer you instead, but I can't find it.

#1. The surest way to help yourself never to tell a primitive lie--a lie to avoid punishment or blame--is to become a saint. If you want advice about that, you will have to read a different book. But even when you have strayed from saintliness in your deeds, you can still hold onto the godliness of your word. To do so means that you need to be willing to risk the punishment that you invited by your deeds and to accept the blame that is rightfully yours.

#2. When you think that people with authority over you would not allow you to do something or to have something that you think you deserve, you will be tempted to seize your forbidden prize and then lie about it. There are essentially two tough alternatives to the telling of entitlement lies: Forgo the pleasure that you feel you deserve, or tell the persons of authority, up-front, that although you know that they object, you are going to do what you please anyway.

#3. Instrumental lies are bold, cold, and manipulative. When you tell such a lie, you have decided that there is something that you want that you can get by lying--maybe a raise, a date, a promotion, or better grade. To refrain from telling such lies, you must decide that your integrity is worth more than money, sex, career advancement, or any other reward.

#4. You have told a lie of honor when you have broken a solemn promise. To help yourself avoid telling lies of honor, consider all promises to be solemn. Remember that most promises are easier to make than to keep. Consider whether you really can and will follow through on your promise. If not, don't risk you honor.

#5. When you fear that your "true" self is just not good enough to impress the important people in your life, you will be tempted to tell a lie about your identity--to simply claim to be the person you wish you were. The cure for this temptation is strong medicine. You need to accept yourself for who you are, or commit to the difficult process of genuine change.

Lessons for Liars:
How to Lie More Humanely

Serious lies are a different domain from the little lies of everyday life. Whereas the little lies are sometimes, in my opinion, excusable or even honorable, there is rarely such dignity in big lies. Still, not everyone will be convinced to forsake their serious lies. This section is for those who plan to go ahead and tell their serious lies anyway, but who would like to do so in the most humane way possible for the people they are deceiving. (If you are telling your lie to be hurtful, you are on your own.)

#1. **Minimize your indiscretions.** Contain the damage. If your misbehavior is in progress, try to stop it. If you cannot stop it, try to slow its rate or narrow its scope and perhaps eventually you will be able to end it.

#2. **Keep your indiscretions to yourself.** Don't perform your misdeeds in public. Flaunting your bad behaviors and your ability to get away with them is risky and cruel. Ultimately, it can prove terribly hurtful to the dupes if they eventually learn that because of your brazenness, everyone else in town knew about your antics before they did. This gratuitous hurtfulness is what you are trying to avoid.

#3. **Keep your lies to yourself.** It might be tempting to enlist co-conspirators in your lies to bolster your sense of adventure and to help you pull off your lies more successfully. It might also be tempting to confide in others about your lies and your misdeeds. Don't do it. The more people who are involved in your lie in any way while the dupes remain oblivious, the more foolish you are making the dupes appear. You are publicly mocking them. More importantly, if and when the targets discover the lie, they will feel all the more hurt, suckered, and outraged if they find that they were betrayed by a whole parade of liars and secret-keepers than if they were victimized by just one scoundrel.

How to Be a Dupe Without Really Trying: Some Warnings

Sometimes dupes are innocent victims of malevolent liars, totally powerless to repel the serious deceptions that are inflicted upon them. But more often than most targets ever imagine, they did have a role in letting the lie happen to them, or even inviting it to happen. In the most obvious instances of this, the dupes collude with the liar to perpetrate the lie, often because they cannot bear to face whatever it is that the lie is hiding. I suspect that often, at some level, colluders know exactly what they are doing.

But dupes can invite others to lie to them in ways that are far more subtle. Not all of these ways are ones that targets will want to do anything about. But it may be enlightening to be aware of them.

#1. **Beware of your own power and authority.**

If you are in command of coveted resources, or if it is your role to dispense perks and privileges, then the people who are dependent on you to obtain these rewards will be tempted to lie to you. Bosses, of course, fit this description beautifully. They can control raises, promotions, work spaces, and company cars, sometimes single-handedly. Parents, too, have enormous power over their children, and because of that power, they also are tremendously tempting targets for their children's lies. Parents have the power to punish as well as to reward their offspring; therefore, they are the most popular targets of the primitive lies told to avoid punishment and blame. Bosses and parents are only the most obvious examples of people with power. Most people have some power over someone, and that power beckons lies.

#2. **Beware of your own sex appeal, beauty, grace, and charm.**

The more appealing you are to other people--sexually, emotionally, or in any other way--the more tempted others will be to tell you lies. The lies elicited by the qualities that make you attractive to other people are among the most flattering lies you will ever be told. These are the lies told to you out of admiration, by people who are so "taken" by you that they feel unworthy in comparison. They lie to make themselves seem a little more appealing to you, because your affection and your regard is so important to them.

Andrew, who fabricated a whole network of connections with important people in town, was trying desperately to impress the worldly couple he so idolized. Paul, the small town boy who felt inadequate next to the other college students who seemed so much more accomplished and sophisticated, lied in hopes of enhancing his value in their discerning eyes. David, who thought he was just a little dork, lied to seem more suave to the very first woman he ever adored. These are not greedy or malicious liars. These people are lying because they like you.

#3. **Beware of the power of your own high expectations.**

When you have high expectations for the behavior of other people, and when you make those expectations clear, the targets of your expectations can feel very flattered. They know you have faith in them. They might also become very motivated to live up to your expectations, and to never let you down. Herein lies the temptation to lie. Most humans, no matter how noble and how deserving of the deepest faith and highest regard, will eventually falter. When they do, it will be most tempting to lie about the misstep to just those persons who will be most surprised by it--those with the deepest faith and highest expectations.

Bertha was a sixth grader who in a moment of anger called her gym teacher a bastard. At the time, she didn't even know what the word meant, although she surmised that it wasn't much of a compliment. Bertha had always been a "good girl"--conscientious, unassuming, and beloved by her teachers, relatives, and friends. To admit to such a bad behavior, she thought, would risk the loss of their fondness and their esteem. So, she lied. She wasn't the only one. If you have high expectations for someone and you let them know it, sooner or later they will probably lie to you.

#4. **Beware of your high moral standards.**

People who loudly proclaim their high moral standards hope that the value they place on honesty and integrity will set an example for others. This is especially so for parents, who hope that their own lofty standards will be honored and internalized by their children. Their goal is to inspire conduct that is decent and noble. But most of the people who hear these paragons of virtue trumpeting their morality are human, and eventually they err. The irony of the trumpeters is that sometimes their blare is so loud and so intimidating that it scares away the truth. People who have strayed from the straight and narrow path would rather admit it to anyone but the righteous ones.

Lucinda was terrified when her father caught her eavesdropping. Instantly, she lied. She owned up to her lie almost as quickly, but by then it was too late. Her guilt for this petty infraction continues to haunt her. Maria's situation was anything but petty. She was a teenager from a deeply religious family who got pregnant and had an abortion. She and her friend Katie were so scared of how such religious parents would react to this truth that they never told it. Instead, they said it was Katie who had the abortion.

Moral standards that are inflexible become clubs that bludgeon others into keeping their unsavory truths to themselves. The moral, I think, is not to value integrity less but to value understanding more.

#5. **Beware of the example you set.**

A great way to encourage others to lie to you is to lie to them. Blatant, manipulative, exploitative lies are especially likely to invite reciprocal mendacity. But so are many more subtle kinds of lies. In some families, for example, parents routinely practice protective lying. They hide from their children for the longest possible time anything that they fear might be distressing to them--an uncle's alcoholism, a pet's irreversible disease, their own plans for divorce, or even more pedestrian sources of anxiety and disappointment, such as the child's appointment with the dentist or the cancellation of the picnic in the park. Parents who create and maintain this family tradition of telling protective lies should not be surprised when their children--including their grown ones--in turn protect *them* from any knowledge of the distressing experiences in their lives.

#6. **Beware of your own vulnerability.**

Diana, the woman who responded to her boyfriend's announcement of his involvement with another woman by running into the bathroom and slitting both wrists, was dramatizing her fragility. Others are much less ostentatious in their displays of vulnerability, but still manage in more subtle ways to convey the message that they will be "broken" by distressing news.

When you announce your vulnerability to other people in subtle or unsubtle ways, you are inviting them to lie to you. Your proclaimed fragility tells them that you just can't handle a painful truth; and so, they just don't tell you the truth. Perhaps your real intent is to dissuade them from ever <u>doing</u> anything that you would find distressing; instead, they may go ahead with their dubious deeds anyway, but just not tell you about them.

Final Note

After pondering all of these pages of sobering truths about serious liars and the people taken in by them, consider this: When my colleagues and I recruited people to tell us about their most profound deceits and dastardly deeds, hardly anyone declined to participate on the grounds that they never told, nor were told, any lies they would consider serious. The tangled web of even the darkest deceptions traps most of us sooner or later.

About the Author

Bella DePaulo (PhD, Harvard) has been studying lying in everyday life for decades. She is the author of more than 100 scholarly publications, many of them on the topic of deception, and is one of the foremost academic experts in the field.

DePaulo's work on deception has been described in the *New York Times*, the *Washington Post*, the *Wall Street Journal*, *USA Today*, and many other major national and international newspapers. It has also been reported in magazines such as *Time*, the *New York Times Magazine*, the *New Yorker*, *Readers' Digest*, and *U.S. News and World Report*. Dr. DePaulo has appeared as an expert on deception on NPR, the *Today Show*, *Good Morning America*, *CBS Sunday Morning*, and other shows on ABC, NBC, CBS, CNN, CNBC, PBS, the BBC, and the Discovery Channel. She has also lectured nationally and internationally. She has addressed criminal attorneys, physicists, judges, and mental health practitioners.

Bella DePaulo is also an expert on the place of people who are single in society and in science. She is the author of *Singled Out: How Singles Are Stereotyped, Stigmatized, and Ignored, and Still Live Happily Ever After* (St. Martin's Press).